"MacNutt is communicating a desperately needed and passionate prophetic call, born of God's eternal Word and rooted in the heart of the Father. Yes! The ministry of healing is intended in the arsenal of power given to us by the Holy Spirit to manifest the relevance of God's love to human pain, just as the message of salvation reveals its answer to human sin. This book is more than timely. It is avant-garde, a 'forerunner' statement among signals I sense the Spirit is sending the Church, saying, *I'm ready to move again in earth-shaking, revival power, ready to move in and through those who will invite My works and wonders.* He wants to glorify Jesus—mighty Savior and loving Healer!"

Jack W. Hayford, chancellor, The King's Seminary;
president, Foursquare Church International

"Francis MacNutt has reached into his vast storehouse of experience to produce a book of extraordinary enlightenment. He skillfully answers the question 'Did prayer for healing disappear without a trace in the Christian churches, or is it alive and well today?' The solution to this mystery is solved in this revealing book. It is destined to become required reading for all seekers of truth."

Barbara Shlemon Ryan, president, Beloved Ministry

"Francis MacNutt's *Nearly Perfect Crime* is a hard-hitting book that should be read by every Christian. Both popular and scholarly, it calls us back to the healing ministry that was almost wiped away from the life of the Church. MacNutt, as much as any other person in modern times, has brought the ministry of healing back to the attention of contemporary Christians in every denomination. I highly recommend this book."

Vinson Synan, dean, School of Divinity, Regent University

"Dr. MacNutt's new book, *The Nearly Perfect Crime,* is an important work for today's Christians. It explains clearly and without theological jargon how the Church lost its healing ministry and how it was regained in the last century. For those of us in the charismatic renewal, it gives us a coherent story of why and how this happened. For those in the mainline churches, it shows that the healing ministry was and is an intrinsic part of the Gospel. This book belongs on the reading list of seminarians, pastors and laypersons alike."

The Rev. William L. De Arteaga, Ph.D., Hispanic rector,
The Light of Christ Anglican Church, Marietta, Ga.

"Francis MacNutt's words, like his healing ministry, forcefully show us how the gift of healing, so powerfully present in the early Church, began to weaken and almost die out, only to rise up time and again. Though forces within and outside the churches have diminished the gift of healing, the Holy Spirit continues to cry out for Christians to reach out and touch the sick and wounded once more today."

Fr. Murray Bodo, O.F.M., author, *Francis: The Journey and the Dream*

"This is *the* book for the whole Church at this critical moment in her history. Out of the maturity of a life poured out to restore the center of Jesus' message and ministry, Francis MacNutt writes with authority, integrity and passion. Our Lord's purpose is summed up in His name and title: As Jesus, He is Savior/Healer; as Christ/Messiah, He is Spirit-empowered. Thus He fulfills His name as He comes to save and heal through the power of the Spirit. For the early centuries this mission was the mission of the Church. It resulted in evangelizing the Roman Empire. But along the way the double reality of healing and the power of the Spirit were largely marginalized and lost. Catholics and Protestants alike receive equal time and equal blame. Thus the almost perfect crime. MacNutt diagnoses with theological and historical narrative both the loss and today's partial recovery. In our remarkable time, Jesus as Healer and the Spirit as Empowerer have become the cutting edge of the Church's worldwide advance. What will restore the Church today, especially in the West? Solving the almost perfect crime and going into action. MacNutt has done it and does it in spades."

Don Williams, Ph.D, author, Vineyard pastor

THE
NEARLY
PERFECT
CRIME

How the Church Almost Killed the Ministry of Healing

FRANCIS MACNUTT

Chosen

Grand Rapids, Michigan

Published by Chosen Books
A division of Baker Publishing Group
P.O. Box 6287, Grand Rapids, MI 49516-6287
www.chosenbooks.com

Printed in the United States of America

Library of Congress Cataloging-in-Publication Data
MacNutt, Francis.
    The nearly perfect crime : how the church almost killed the ministry of healing / Francis MacNutt.
        p.   cm.
    Includes bibliographical references and index.
    ISBN 0-8007-9390-0 (cloth)
    1. Spiritual healing—History of doctrines. I. Title.
BT732.5.M336 2005
234'.131—dc22   2004022348

To Judith,
my beloved wife
devoted mother of Rachel and David
loyal, encouraging and inspired companion
in the journey to
better understand Jesus' passion to heal.
And to all those pioneers who showed me the way,
among whom were
Rev. Tommy Tyson,
Agnes Sanford
and
John Wimber.

CONTENTS

ACKNOWLEDGMENTS

In a very special way I want to thank our secretary, Mrs. Gail Mosely, who not only typed this manuscript but made many helpful editorial suggestions. She also shielded me from many of the inevitable interruptions that break the quiet I needed to write.

Also, in a special way, Jane Campbell, Chosen Books editor, who has worked with me on several books and whose advice I seek when I run into a question of what to include in the vast subject I have attempted to approach in this book. Her unfailing cheerfulness as well as editorial wisdom always encourage me when I phone her for suggestions.

Over the years, too, my dear friend, the late Rev. Tommy Tyson, was like a brother to me and we often talked over the fascinating topic that is at the heart of *The Nearly Perfect Crime*.

INTRODUCTION

I want to write as simply as possible, stating my point clearly in order to help the Church return to an essential part of the life that Jesus Christ came to give us.

The point is simply this: Jesus came to bring us healing (and deliverance) on every level of our being—physical, emotional and spiritual—through the power of the Holy Spirit. As Peter summed up Christ's ministry: "God had anointed him with the Holy Spirit and with power, and because God was with him, Jesus went about doing good and curing all who had fallen into the power of the devil" (Acts 10:38, JB).

This teaching is central to the Gospel; it is not a side issue. But over the centuries a lively belief in healing prayer was taken away, not only by the enemies of Christianity, but, surprisingly, by Christians themselves. We are not dealing with villains here but good, even holy leaders who nearly killed Christian healing; the monks, for instance, fled to the desert (ca. A.D. 400) to escape the sinful cities and then refused, in the name of humility, to pray for the sick.

As a result, by the opening of the twentieth century healing prayer had largely disappeared from the mainline historic Church. This has been a tragic loss: The full expression of Jesus' main ministry has, by and large, remained lost to the traditional centers of Christianity. That is a bold statement, but it needs to be set out in plain view, in its stark outline, so we can come to realize that we have accepted "the traditions of men" rather than the authentic traditions of Christianity. You may be surprised, perhaps even angered, at what this book contains. All I ask is that you read with an open mind, an open heart and an open spirit.

See if it's not true.

In stating my case—which I believe is the case of the Gospel—I will not write with a multitude of subtle distinctions and a profusion of scholarly references. The main points need to stand out boldly so that all of us in the Body of Christ can recapture His vision and begin to work together toward a serious renewal of Christian life.

If you disagree with this or that point, fine. But if the main sweep of this book is true, we need to repent—individually and as a Church—and then change our lives and try to live according to Jesus' original vision.

PART 1

A CHRISTIAN
MANIFESTO

1

THE NEARLY PERFECT CRIME

They will keep up the outward appearance of religion but will have rejected the inner power of it.

2 Timothy 3:5, JB

It was a nearly perfect crime.

You can see the body lying there, almost cold, the heart barely pumping. This dying body once kept Christianity alive. What we see lying there, scarcely moving, is Christian prayer for healing.

It is like the lingering death of the emperor Napoleon, in exile on the Isle of Elba. According to the story, the English paid his servant to put a pinch of arsenic in Napoleon's wine every evening. Day by day he wasted away until he finally died. We can compare the near-death of Christian healing to Napoleon's sad decline, except that its decline was even more gradual.

Century by century its life was weakened; by 1900 only certain parts of the Church's healing ministry were still alive and moving. Granted, something so central to Christianity could never completely die; we can rejoice that Christians today in different parts of the world are awakening to the glorious vision that Jesus had for His Church. But, amazingly, most of the body lies still and unresponsive to the powerful encounters of the Spirit that are sweeping into these "nontraditional" meetings of believers. So stealthily did this poisoning happen that most churchgoers did not even realize that anything was wrong. They came to think of their moribund state as normal.

When you think about it, this near-destruction of divine healing is an extraordinary mystery, because miraculous healing—with its twin, the casting out of evil spirits—lay at the very heart of Jesus Christ's mission. For the first four hundred years of Church history Christians expected healing to take place when they prayed! How is it possible that something so central to the Gospel almost died out?

The mystery is compounded when we discover that the enemies were not outsiders or heretics, but Christians themselves. It is as if Christians put a pinch of arsenic into their own wine day after day and then drank it. Well-meaning Christians—leaders and theologians—made prayer for healing a side issue. In weakening this central teaching of the Gospel, they unwittingly opened themselves to the influence of paganism, Platonism, Stoicism and Gnosticism.

Ironically, these devout Christians thought they were acting as servants of truth and could not see that they were harming their own cause. It reminds us of the religious leaders of Jesus' day who were convinced they were doing the right thing in handing Jesus over to die upon a cross: "It was expedient," they said (John 18:14, KJV).

It is as if Satan called together a council of the subtlest and most clever demons and asked, "How can we rob Christians of the very life that Jesus came to give them? How can we encourage them to build monuments to their past glory, all the while sucking the life out of today's Church? I don't care how long it takes. We have already succeeded in killing the Christ; we hung Him up naked outside His beloved city and pierced His heart. Now it's time to finish the job and take the heart out of His other Body, the Church."

The Church's original healing ministry was so strong and vital, so clearly a part of the Gospel, that the crime could not take place all at once. It took time—nearly two thousand years. Still the enemies of healing succeeded so well that by 1970 an accepted spiritual author could claim that "miracles are merely a holdover from the age of pre-scientific explanation, an anachronism which persists only in those moldering ivory towers which continue to exist."[1]

Notice I have mentioned that the crime was not perfect—only nearly perfect. There was still enough belief among the common people that even centuries of trying by spiritual leaders and authorities could not squelch it. In fact, in the past hundred years we have seen an amazing resurrection of the healing ministry—generally among the "ordinary" people—and later we will talk about that. But mostly, in the established churches healing has become a lost gift. And not only lost, but ridiculed: *Faith healer* has become a term of reproach.

As a result, millions of suffering Christians—and nonbelievers as well—who could have been healed remained sick, and many have died before their time. St. Paul did not hesitate to say that many Christians were weak or had even died because they did not recognize the Body of Christ (see 1 Corinthians 11:30). The victims are real. You may know this all too well. Perhaps you are suffering from a sickness from which you could be healed if only you had better understanding about healing prayer.

In a fascinating turn of events, science has pointed a light on the Church's loss of vision: Several medical case studies have shown that prayer helps in the healing process. Larry Dossey, M.D., makes an interesting observation: "Will we reach a point where physicians who ignore prayer will be judged guilty of malpractice?"[2] If a medical doctor can talk about suing his fellow physicians, what might we say about priests and ministers who do not pray for healing when the Gospel is "their territory," as it were? Are they not also guilty of malpractice, not for what they do, but—like the doctors—for what they fail to do?

As I mentioned earlier, the work of casting out evil spirits is always partner to prayers for healing. Over the centuries this ministry of deliverance[3] has also been neglected and scorned until it has nearly died out as well. Heads turned when the chief exorcist of Rome, Father Gabriele Amorth, was bold enough to write:

> I am convinced that allowing the ministry of exorcism to die is an unforgiveable deficiency to be laid squarely at the door of bishops. Every diocese should have at least one exorcist at the cathedral, and every large parish and sanctuary should have one as well. Today the exorcist is seen as a rarity, almost impossible to find. . . . I do not hesitate to repeat what I have written elsewhere: if a bishop, when faced with a valid request for an exorcism—I am not talking about the request of some demented per-

son—does not address the problem, either personally or by delegating the task to a qualified priest, he is guilty of a most serious sin of omission.[4]

How is it possible that this partnership of healing and deliverance, this central mission of Christianity aside from preaching, almost disappeared? On the other hand, it is just as amazing that the healing ministry survived as strongly as it did, considering how, century after century, powerful forces were at work to engineer its demise.

This is the mystery we will investigate. It is an incredible, fascinating story and one that must be told for the health of the Body because these disabling elements are still among us. I believe that Jesus desires with all His heart for His saving love, revealed through healing and deliverance, to return to His people full force.

2

THERE HAS TO BE MORE!

Back in the 1960s, when I was a young Catholic priest, one of the things that discouraged me was trying to give spiritual direction to a number of sincere, committed Christians who were suffering from a number of difficult personal problems. Some were severely depressed, some struggled with addictions, some erupted with irrational anger. Like so many other priests and ministers, I encouraged them not to lose heart but to keep on trying. My suggestions mostly had to do with strengthening their willpower to conquer their destructive inclinations. Being inventive, I tried to develop creative methods of coping. Sometimes these people got better but, sadly, the most deeply wounded did well just to hang on to life.

A number of these individuals were actively suicidal. They told me about the methods they planned to use to end their lives, such as overdosing on pills, if their emotional pain grew too strong. Now, I was not trying to help these hurting souls by myself; I made referrals to connect them with mental health counselors and several came to me because their psychiatrist had suggested me as a spiritual director.

Most of my training in spirituality had concentrated on repenting of sin, on regaining a positive vision of God's love and on strengthening

19

willpower. But I quickly discovered the limits of human willpower, although I always added, "You need God's grace to help you."

So what was the answer? It was hard enough for suffering people to handle their pain on the human level, but on the spiritual level what advice was I supposed to give? Were some people so badly wounded by their past experiences (such as repeated incest by their fathers) that they were truly hopeless? Some hated life. They hated themselves and they suspected that God hated them, too. They asked me hard questions: "Do you really think God would condemn me if I killed myself? You know my past and that there's nothing I can do to change it. I've seen a psychiatrist for years now and I'm still not better. Do you really believe anything will ever change? I'm already fifty years old and, from now on, it's all going downhill. Do you really think I'll ever get better?"

In all honesty I couldn't say yes. If they had not gotten better from their psychiatric treatments, from their medications, from their electric-shock therapy, what else could I offer them? Was it true that a large group of people out there were spiritually hopeless? Could they never be happy? Was I just wasting my time?

One woman who came to see me said, "I'm not Marianne[1] who has a disease, but I'm a disease named Marianne." How do you even begin to deal with something like that? (I repeat that these people were already receiving professional mental and medical help.)

About this time several other priests on our faculty (I was teaching in our Dominican seminary in Dubuque, Iowa) started questioning me about all the time I spent "holding hands with a bunch of nuts" (as one teaching colleague described it). I was being called to the phone constantly to help with the needs of my counselees and it was becoming a nuisance. The regent of studies warned me that all of this time spent with troubled human beings was distracting me from the time I should be spending preparing for class and working with our seminarians. I knew he was right.

But I also knew that just an hour's visit every two weeks seemed to be enough to keep a suicidal person alive. At one point I had to leave Dubuque for two weeks and, while I was away, two of my counselees attempted suicide. Spending time with these hurting people seemed to give them just enough attention to help them want to live. How could I tell them, "I'm not going to see you any more"?

Aside from the personal dilemma I was facing, I could not escape the fact that the problem was larger in scope. The big question was directed not only to me as an individual but also to the larger Christian community, to the Church. Are we meant to work only with the well adjusted? That just didn't seem right.

The best answer most of the Church had for the very real question of suffering and pain—Job's question—was that it is an ordinary part of human life, which is certainly true. If suffering is unavoidable, then, we should help one another endure our pain, our "cross," with courage and patience in this life, and we will be rewarded in the next life. Our community edited a journal on spirituality, *Cross and Crown*, whose very title illustrated the prevalence of this teaching: If you endure your suffering in union with the suffering of Jesus, you will receive a crown in heaven.

Now, I believe this is largely true; there is such a thing as redemptive suffering, and we will not escape suffering in this life. But at the same time many people, including many devoted Christians, are enduring the kind of sickness—especially emotional sickness—that leads them to despair. Their pain is not proving to be redemptive.

This is why I heard desperation in the voices of my counselees. They were asking questions that I think any honest person would also ask: "Where is God in all this? Does He really *love* me? I only have proof that He doesn't love me—my entire life shows that He doesn't love me. Maybe He loves you but I'm damaged beyond repair."

I remember teaching at a retreat conference once where I asked those in attendance to draw pictures representing what they felt about themselves. One woman drew a picture of herself as a blind eagle. Another pictured herself as a skunk. Where do you go from there? What was the Christian answer? For them repentance and willpower were not enough.

Thus I was reluctant, in spite of the skepticism of some of my fellow teachers, to give up the one thing I had discovered that helped: Really caring about these hurting people seemed to enable them to survive. Many others were making the same discovery. It certainly didn't cure their sufferings but it helped.

Yet here again I had problems. A major one, of course, was keeping appropriate distance from those under my spiritual care—and not only physical distance but emotional distance. All professional and spiritual

counselors are taught, of course, to remain alert to the emotional bond-
ing issues known as "transference" and "counter-transference." We in
the priesthood were trained to stay detached, while remaining kind.
Then, after listening, we were to offer some practical advice. It was as
if the mind alone was to be engaged and that seemed to make good
sense. Emotions only got in the way and clouded one's judgment.

The only problem was that if you really cared about a person, he or
she would likely become attached to you, especially if the person had
been deeply rejected and wounded in life. The fact that someone cared
even a little became greatly magnified. Several of my counselees told
me that the only reason they had not committed suicide during the
previous week was because they didn't want to hurt or sadden me.

So, while maintaining appropriate boundaries, I gradually came
to realize that the love and concern I showed them was more healing
than any advice I could give. In other words, the emotional part of
any spiritual direction I had to offer was probably more important
than any advice my mind could generate. You just cannot separate
the mind and the heart.

Nor did they seem to be getting help anywhere else. Even expensive
psychiatric sessions had their limits.

So I continued to wonder how all this fit into Christianity. Were
there vast numbers of people who, as Thoreau observed, were doomed
to live their lives in quiet desperation? That did not seem to fit the Gospel. Were we simply destined to be chaplains to the well adjusted?

Then I read a revolutionary book by a psychiatrist named William Glasser, who disagreed strongly with Freud's detached approach:
"Well-meaning advice always fails—patients can't straighten up and
fly right when someone points out reality to them when there is not
sufficient involvement. . . . Psychiatry must be concerned with two
basic psychological needs: *the need to love and be loved and the need
to feel that we are worthwhile to ourselves and to others*."[2] He went on
to explain his discovery that he could not really help people unless
he became involved in their lives.

Now, this was exactly what I was finding. But it created huge practical problems for me. It might be fine for professional counselors to
spend large amounts of time with a few clients, but that was not what
I was called to do. Nor did I have the training. And yet it became
clearer and clearer that most people in this world were crying out for

compassion, and they were dying spiritually and emotionally because they did not receive it in a healthy way.

It is a psychological law that we need to be loved into being. Similarly, Jesus' great command in the Gospel is that we are supposed to love each other as He has loved us. Why wasn't it happening? What was missing? What was the answer?

There had to be more to Christianity than what I had so far discovered.

What that "more" was I would only learn many years later.

PART 2

THE WAY
WE WERE

3

OUR LONG LOST INHERITANCE

As we investigate the heart of the Christian message and how we have lost a large part of it, I think the best way to start is at the beginning, with God's original plan. We will remain forever in the dark if we do not understand *why* God sent His Son to be Savior of the world. Why did Jesus come among us in the flesh? He came because we had lost our inheritance and He intended to restore it.

What inheritance did we lose? The answer to this question actually predates Jesus' earthly life and ministry. Let's begin then with three key teachings from Scripture.

1. God's Creation Is "Good"

The first great teaching of the Hebrew Scriptures, the Old Testament, gives us God's view of His creation: In the beginning God created everything that exists and He saw that it was *good* (see Genesis 1:1–30). And, taken in its totality, the universe was *very good* (see verse 31).

The initial creation was marvelously good! All human beings, represented by Adam and Eve, were part of this wonderful creation and were meant to be specially blessed. This Hebrew teaching ran counter to the beliefs of many pagan religions; they emphasized that creation was evil and that the gods of evil were equal to the good God and needed to be appeased and worshiped.

2. The Human Race Falls into Sin

The second great teaching is that there has been a *Fall*, and that Satan helped cause it (see Genesis 3:1–24). In whatever way Christians understand the story of the Fall, whether we view it literally or allegorically, the basic point is that, through pride, the human race sinned and fell from fellowship with its Creator. The disastrous consequence was that evil came into the world and now influences everything in it. Because of the Fall, every human being still experiences a radical wounding.

> To the woman he said, "I will greatly increase your pains in childbearing; with pain you will give birth to children. Your desire will be for your husband, and he will rule over you."
> To Adam he said, "Because you listened to your wife and ate from the tree about which I commanded you, 'You must not eat of it,' cursed is the ground because of you; through painful toil you will eat of it all the days of your life. It will produce thorns and thistles for you, and you will eat the plants of the field. By the sweat of your brow you will eat your food until you return to the ground, since from it you were taken; for dust you are and to dust you will return."
>
> Genesis 3:16–19

Just as the Creation was fully good, the Fall was fully catastrophic—and very, very real. You may be aware of a disagreement in Christian tradition on the "depth" of our Fall. Roman Catholicism, for instance, holds that humans are "badly wounded" while Calvinism maintains that we are "totally corrupt." Whatever our position on the scale of depravity, our condition remains tragic. As Cardinal Newman observed, all you need to do is look around and see that something is dreadfully wrong with the human race.

Disasters cut across every aspect of our lives, "mourning and weeping in this valley of tears." And the grief cuts even deeper when we understand that these evils are too great for us to overcome by our own abilities. As Paul wrote: "Our struggle is not against flesh and blood, but against the rulers, against the authorities, against the powers of this dark world and against the spiritual forces of evil in the heavenly realms" (Ephesians 6:12). In recent centuries, these verses have often been interpreted as symbol rather than fact, but to Paul and the early Church, these demonic forces were real and bent on our destruction.

Among the tragedies that weigh upon us as a result of our Fall, the following are four of the most notable:

Estrangement from God

God now seems far off; we are outside the Garden, as it were, and can't get back in. It reminds me of my visits to areas of Africa where the "great God," "the High God," is viewed by the pagans as a good God. Yet they see Him as so distant they don't bother much with Him: He won't hurt them. The ones they worry about are the ones who influence this earth, who curse people and make them sick—these are the demons whom they need to appease through sacrifice. To deal with these evil forces, the pagans turn to their native witch doctors who have power in the unseen world and can "protect" them. At a cost!

The Rulership of Satan

The whole world is now somehow under the dominion of Satan. While tempting Jesus, Satan took Him to a high mountain and showed Him the kingdoms of the world and their splendor. "'All this I will give you,' he said, 'if you will bow down and worship me'" (Matthew 4:9). Notice that Satan assumed that the kingdoms of the world were under his dominion and he now dominated this world. Nor did Jesus contradict him. The gospels and epistles confirm this bleak view of the natural universe. "We know that we are children of God, and that the whole world is under the control of the evil one" (1 John 5:19).

The Inclination to Sin

We human beings are deeply affected by the Fall in every dimension of our humanity and are *inclined to sin*: "I do not understand what I do. For what I want to do I do not do, but what I hate I do" (Romans 7:15).

These effects include:

- weakness in our *wills*, making it hard for us to resist sin
- blindness in our *minds*, making it easy for us to mistake error for truth
- chaos in our *emotions*, drawing us into sin through anger, through fear, through lust and all the other emotional drives that influence us
- sickness in our *bodies*, some of it through our own fault, but most of it just inherent in our fallen human condition
- and, finally, the last enemy of all, *death*

Macro Effects of Sin

In our society and culture, and even on the world level, we see large-scale effects of the Fall, notably in wars and in the oppression of the weak and the poor.

3. A New Creation Arises

The third great teaching of the Scriptures is that our humanity is meant to become a *new creation*. Aside from healing the wounded part of the old creation and destroying the evil powers that enslave us, the positive news of the Gospel is not just that the old creation is being restored to what it once was, but that a whole new creation is now here. Paul explained it: "If anyone is in Christ, he is a new creation; the old has gone, the new has come! All this is from God" (2 Corinthians 5:17–18).

There are three key components of this new creation which truly make the Gospel great news!

First, the greatest gift of all that Jesus came to bring *is a new relationship with God, with the King.* The distant God, who was believed to exist in a distant heaven, now comes to live not just with us, but within us. As Jesus said to His followers on the night before He died:

> "I will not leave you as orphans; I will come to you. Before long, the world will not see me anymore, but you will see me. Because I live, you also will live. On that day you will realize that I am in my Father, and you are in me, and I am in you."
>
> John 14:18–20

Breaking down that distance is the greatest gift of all. Now we are not only enabled to *know about God*, but in some mysterious way, we are enabled *to know God* in our own experience. St. Thomas Aquinas (writing in the thirteenth century) summarized early Christian tradition when he stated that the greatest prophecy foretelling the New Covenant, the New Testament, was proclaimed by the prophet Jeremiah when he wrote:

> "This is the covenant I will make with the house of Israel after that time," declares the Lord. "I will put my law in their minds and write it on their hearts. I will be their God, and they will be my people. No longer will a man teach his neighbor, or a man his brother, saying, 'Know the Lord,' because they will all know me, from the least of them to the greatest," declares the Lord.
>
> Jeremiah 31:33–34

Second, *we become a new kind of person.* Another great gift, not often appreciated or preached, is that, through the power of the Spirit, we are personally meant to become a new, wonderfully alive, kind of person. Paul describes what we are meant to become: loving, patient, kind, gentle, never jealous, rude or selfish. We can always delight in the truth, always be ready to excuse, to trust and to endure whatever comes (see 1 Corinthians 13:4–7).

Third, *the wounded world is restored.* The main reason Jesus came as Savior was to reverse this tragic situation and transform our fallen world and place it back in the Kingdom of God. In His nature miracles, we see Jesus healing even our wounded natural world. Not only does

He heal sick human beings, but He also heals the wounded world of nature that is now out of order and has fallen along with the human race.

> He got up, rebuked the wind and said to the waves, "Quiet! Be still!" Then the wind died down and it was completely calm. He said to his disciples, "Why are you so afraid? Do you still have no faith?" They were terrified and asked each other, "Who is this? Even the wind and the waves obey him!"
>
> Mark 4:39–41

Why God's Plan Remains an "Ideal"

God intends us to become a new kind of human being, truly loving and unselfish. Sadly, our experience often contradicts this beautiful ideal. The Crusades, the persecutions of the Jews, the killing conflicts in Northern Ireland seem to prove that most Christians don't seem to be any better than anyone else. Gandhi saw right through the Christians he knew in South Africa and India, and he was not impressed. He applauded Christian principles, but not Christians. Over the centuries our dismal record stands as an embarrassment.

Why is it that Christians are not all that different? Why is the number of divorces among Christians in the United States almost the same as among people who have no Christian affiliation? Why are the marriages of pastors breaking up nearly as frequently as those of laypeople? Young people ask the obvious question: "Does it make any difference whether or not I am Christian?"

My mother, a naturally outgoing, loving person, dropped out of her childhood church with all of her seven brothers and sisters because of their disillusion at what they perceived as a lack of love. They were all young when their father died in a fire and their mother, soon after, died of typhoid fever. Their grandmother stepped up to the challenge and reared all eight of them. Not surprisingly, they had to dress in hand-me-downs, and when a few busybodies in the congregation made snide remarks about how poorly they were dressed, the entire family dropped out of church and none of the eight ever went back.

I was always concerned about my mother's never having any desire to belong to a church, although she never objected to my going to the Roman Catholic Church with my dad and sister. It worried me. Every so often, when I was in college, I would invite her to come with me to church to hear some eloquent priest give a sermon. Contrary to my hopes, she would always pay more attention to watching the people in the pews than listening to the sermon. After the service was over, she would usually say something like, "But Franz (her nickname for me), the people in church don't look very happy. And they don't look as though they care about each other." And what could I say to that? (I realize that there are numerous churches where the people are remarkably friendly, especially in relating to newcomers. I'm speaking here about the church in which I grew up.)

Finally, in 1968, when we had started a charismatic prayer group that quickly grew to three hundred people who met at Visitation Academy in St. Louis, I again invited her to come. This time, she saw something different. The next day she told me, "Now, Franz, that's what religion is all about! Those people love each other."

I realized I could not fault her for using the same criterion that Jesus had set out: "By this love you have for one another, everyone will know that you are my disciples"(John 13:35, JB). For her, loving people was far more important than believing correct doctrine. She was looking for a loving church rather than a dogmatically true church.

I find that countless other people have dropped out of their churches for the same reason. At the time I am writing this, many Roman Catholics are furious and grief-stricken to learn that some priests are guilty of sexual crimes against children. Church attendance among Roman Catholics has dropped an astounding 11 percent in one year.

Church officials are making a defense, claiming that the incidence of pedophilia is probably not greater among priests than among adult males in the population at large. But that in itself is a sad commentary. If being a Christian means anything in real life, the incidence of sex abuse among Christians should be all but nonexistent. So again we ask: Why isn't it? Why is our behavior no better, statistically, than nonbelievers'?

God wants to transform us into a new creation so that we can become part of His own family. But we are besieged by all kinds of evils that prevent us from achieving the great purpose for which God created us. Without healing, without deliverance from evil, without God's help, we will never regain our inheritance. All of these are imperative. Without them we will never fully achieve our destiny of becoming a new creation. But there is another condition as well.

We cannot live the Gospel ideal without the power of the Holy Spirit. When Paul talked about a new creation, he was not just mouthing a beautiful concept, a pious abstraction. To him the new creation was very real because he knew through his own experience that he could live in this revolutionary way only if he continually experienced God's help. The power of the Spirit is not just an idea, a teaching that we accept; it is a real force that can change our lives.

In Paul's letter to the Romans, he described his own sobering experience:

> We know that the law is spiritual; but I am unspiritual, sold as a slave to sin. I do not understand what I do. For what I want to do I do not do, but what I hate I do. And if I do what I do not want to do, I agree that the law is good. As it is, it is no longer I myself who do it, but it is sin living in me. I know that nothing good lives in me, that is, in my sinful nature. For I have the desire to do what is good, but I cannot carry it out. For what I do is not the good I want to do; no, the evil I do not want to do—this I keep on doing.
>
> Romans 7:14–19

Here we find the key to this mystery as to why, over the centuries, we Christians have exhibited such a miserable group record (with a few exceptions). It is not enough for us just to believe in some beautiful ideal: God intends for us to live in that glorious way and we just cannot do it—not without the help of the Holy Spirit.

God's Plan to Redeem Us

It was God's plan from the beginning to help us. He knew that we would not be able to reclaim our inheritance on our own. So, in His mercy, God chose the Israelites to come apart and learn about Him and His plan. They were to start out by worshiping the One True God and were instructed to follow some basic commandments—most especially to take care of the weak and the poor.

Jewish history describes an all-too-human story of a few noble kings mixed in with a majority of evil kings who constantly led the Israelites into disastrous decisions. God kept sending prophets to warn them to stay on the right path, but false prophets also arose and the people veered off course once more. But in the midst of God's dealings with His oft-rebellious people, He prepared them to look forward to a Messiah who would lead them, and the entire world, to freedom.

In the time of Jesus, many attached their own political agendas onto their image of the Messiah, envisioning Him as a military leader who, like David, would form a powerful army to free the Israelites from the harsh oppression of Rome. Instead of responding to these political dreams, Jesus went far deeper, touching the deep roots of our human dilemma by fulfilling the Suffering Servant prophecies in Isaiah. He was a Messiah who would take the evil of the world into Himself and cut to the very base of our human problems: our inability to love—in particular, our refusal to love our enemies. Instead of riding into Jerusalem triumphantly on a white steed, He rode in, unarmed, on a donkey.

> Surely he took up our infirmities and carried our sorrows, yet we considered him stricken by God, smitten by him, and afflicted. But he was pierced for our transgressions, he was crushed for our iniquities; the punishment that brought us peace was upon him, and by his wounds we are healed.
>
> Isaiah 53:4–5

This is the theme of Christianity, that we need a Savior—and not just a great teacher. Only God can rescue us with His own ability to overcome the evil that has overpowered us for thousands of years. We learn from the Scriptures that, even though we may have been given true teaching, we still are miserable failures at trying to live up to these great ideals. "I do what I hate doing" is Paul's summary of the human dilemma.

To our surprise, God then sent His own Son, a human being like us in every way, except sin (see Hebrews 4:15). He went through all the pain that we still suffer because of our fallen human condition, but then, empowered by the Holy Spirit, He frees us from the evils that resulted from the Fall and restores our inheritance:

- In place of our estrangement from His Father, He bestows on us *forgiveness* and *reconciliation*; we even become members of His family.
- In place of our weakness, He fills us with His own *Holy Spirit*— His own power.
- For our blindness, He gives us spiritual *enlightenment* through the same Holy Spirit.
- In place of the chaos in our emotions, He *heals our broken hearts*.
- To replace our physical sickness, He *heals our bodies*.
- To combat our inclination to go to war and to oppress the weak, He shares His love and compassion through the *fruits of His Spirit*.
- And He even overcomes the last enemy, death, by *raising the dead* to life.

These miracles of God's love and power are the reality that confirms our preaching when we dare to proclaim the impossible dream—that "the Kingdom of God is in your midst; the kingdom of Satan is being destroyed." Without the power of God that makes healing and deliverance from evil actually happen, our preaching remains mere theory and does not touch the *reality* of our wretched lives. Instead of preaching Good News, we end up preaching good advice.

The only dimension of this freeing message that is still very much alive is that we can be reconciled with God and that God forgives our sins. That, certainly, is the most important element but so much of the rest has disappeared. Certainly, the lives of most Christians do not display the radiant difference that should make us stand out from the unhappy world around us.

Healing: A Key Part of God's Plan

The basic practical heresy in present-day Christianity is that we act as if we can cure our own problems and the problems of the world through our own intelligence and effort. Long ago this attitude ("Pelagianism") was labeled as a heresy. We still talk about grace and believe in it theoretically, but the Bible tells us that we are fallen—blind, weak, violent—the characteristics that Paul enumerates as the work of the "flesh" (see Galatians 5:16–26, KJV).[1]

Long before the Messiah appeared, God was already working to repair the ravages of sickness plaguing the human race. We read about how the prophet Elijah raised the son of the widow of Zarephath back to life (see 1 Kings 17:17–24; Luke 4:26) and how God used Elisha to heal the Syrian general, Naaman, of his leprosy (see 2 Kings 5:14; Luke 4:27).

Throughout, the Hebrew Scriptures show us a vision of healing that is to come in Messianic times. Take, for example, this beautiful passage in Isaiah:

> Strengthen the feeble hands, steady the knees that give way; say to those with fearful hearts, "Be strong, do not fear; your God will come, he will come with vengeance; with divine retribution he will come to save you." Then will the eyes of the blind be opened and the ears of the deaf unstopped. Then will the lame leap like a deer, and the mute tongue shout for joy.
>
> Isaiah 35:3–6

Isaiah presents God as caring for us even more than a human mother would: "Can a mother forget the baby at her breast and have no compassion on the child she has borne? Though she may forget, I will not forget you! See, I have engraved you on the palms of my hands" (Isaiah 49:15–16).

Is this loss of vision and spiritual power the reason that the history of Christianity has shown such violence, such blindness, such division? Have we simply not known what God has bestowed on us?

God had an answer for lost humanity and it was to send a Messiah, someone to restore our heritage.

His name would be Jesus, and He would be known as the Christ.

4

"And His Name Shall Be Called . . ."

What was in God's mind when He sent His Son to live among us? The best place to answer this question is in finding out why God named Him *Jesus* even before He was born. Jesus' name declares God's meaning for His life.

The Hebrew people believed that a child's name affected the child's destiny and mission in life, so parents were very serious about seeking God's guidance when the time came to choose a name for a newborn.

We remember, for example, how much turmoil ensued when the parents of John the Baptist were getting ready to name him.

> They were going to name him after his father Zechariah, but his mother spoke up and said, "No! He is to be called John."[1] They said to her, "There is no one among your relatives who has that name."
>
> Then they made signs to his father, to find out what he would like to name the child. He asked for a writing tablet, and to everyone's astonishment he wrote, "His name is John." Immediately his mouth was opened and his tongue was loosed, and he began to speak, praising God. The

neighbors were all filled with awe, and throughout the hill country of
Judea people were talking about all these things.

Luke 1:59–65

To view another example, we recall that the destiny of Jacob was
foreshadowed by his name, which means "supplanter." Scripture tells
us how he actually took the place of Esau, his elder brother. Esau
lamented, "Isn't he rightly named Jacob? He has deceived me these
two times: He took my birthright, and now he's taken my blessing!"
(Genesis 27:36).

Sometimes God even changed a person's name, which meant that
He was also changing his or her destiny. The great patriarch, for example, started out in life as Abram, but when he was 99 years old
God appeared to him and said, "No longer will you be called Abram;
your name will be Abraham, for I have made you a father of many
nations. I will make you very fruitful; I will make nations of you, and
kings will come from you" (Genesis 17:5–6). Likewise, Sarai became
Sarah, a mother of nations.

Then there is the famous example of how Jesus renamed Simon
Bar Jona after he had confessed that Jesus was the Christ, the Son of
the living God:

> "I tell you that you are Peter, and on this rock I will build my church, and
> the gates of Hades will not overcome it. I will give you the keys of the
> kingdom of heaven; whatever you bind on earth will be bound in heaven,
> and whatever you loose on earth will be loosed in heaven."
>
> Matthew 16:18–19

As you know, *Peter* (Greek: *petros*; Aramaic: *kepha*) means "rock." Jesus
was signifying that from this point on, Peter was to be like a rock of
strength upon which He could build His Church.[2]

Knowing the high value the Jewish people attached to naming a
child, we can imagine that Mary and Joseph might not have been
surprised that God, who was giving this Son, also named Him. God
sent the angel Gabriel to Mary with this announcement:

> "You will be with child and give birth to a son, and you are to give him the
> name Jesus. He will be great and will be called the Son of the Most High.

The Lord God will give him the throne of his father David, and he will
reign over the house of Jacob forever; his kingdom will never end."

Luke 1:31–33

After Jesus' birth, on the day of His circumcision, "he was named
Jesus, the name the angel had given him before he had been conceived"
(Luke 2:21). The translation of His name (Hebrew: *Jeshua*) is "God
saves" or "God heals," and this signified His God-given mission in life.
For the Hebrews, who did not divide people into component parts to
the extent we do, *healing* and *saving* meant basically the same thing.
So whenever we say the name *Jesus*, we are also saying that His main
mission was to heal and to save.

In Matthew's gospel, this connection between His name and His
mission was actually affirmed. Before Jesus' birth an angel also appeared to Joseph and said that Mary would bear a son. Then he gave
Joseph this direction: "You are to give him the name Jesus, because
he will save his people from their sins" (Matthew 1:21).

Like most children of the day, Jesus had only one name—not like us
with middle and last names. To distinguish Him from other men who
were also named Jesus, He was simply known as "Jesus the carpenter's
son" or "the son of Joseph" or "Jesus of Nazareth."

Christ was His title, but it was not His name (He was not ordinarily
called "Jesus, the Christ" in His lifetime). It means "the anointed one,"
deriving from the Greek *christos*. In His first sermon, Jesus stated that
"the Spirit of the Lord is on me, because he has anointed me" (Luke
4:18). He was claiming to be the Christ, the one who was anointed
with the Spirit, the Messiah.

This anointing of the Spirit gave Jesus God's power to accomplish
His mission. That mission was saving, healing and rescuing people
from their sins, their sicknesses and their bondage to evil.

At the end of Jesus' life, Peter summed it all up one more time: "God
had anointed him with the Holy Spirit and with power[3] [the Christ],
and because God was with him, Jesus went about doing good and curing all who had fallen into the power of the devil" (Acts 10:38, JB).

Every time we say the name *Jesus*, we are declaring our faith in His
mission: He is the one who heals, who saves.

Every time we say the title *Christ*, we are declaring our belief in the source of His power to heal: the Holy Spirit.

And now we move forward to examine the life of Jesus, the Messiah, and see how He Himself viewed healing and exorcism as key parts of His own mission to rescue the human race.

5

HOW DID JESUS SEE
HIS MISSION?

As we continue our journey, understanding God's desire to help us regain our lost inheritance of healing prayer, the next place to start is with Jesus Himself. How important was healing to Jesus and why?

What was *Jesus' own vision* of His personal mission?

Jesus made it easy for us to grasp that vision because He made Isaiah's prophecy His own when He came to Nazareth, right after He was filled with the power of the Spirit (see Luke 3:21–22; 4:1–2, 14). In Luke's gospel this was Jesus' first proclamation, laying out the basic program for His life's work. In terms of our own national experience, it was like His "state of the union" address, laying out the program for His entire life. Standing up in the synagogue in His hometown of Nazareth, He unrolled the scroll of the prophet Isaiah and read out the section where this was written:

"The Spirit of the Lord is on me, because he has anointed me to preach good news to the poor. He has sent me to proclaim freedom for the prisoners and recovery of sight for the blind, to release the oppressed, to proclaim the year of the Lord's favor." Then he rolled up the scroll, gave it back to the attendant and sat down. The eyes of everyone in the synagogue were fastened on him, and he began by saying to them, "Today this scripture is fulfilled in your hearing."

Luke 4:18–21

The rest of Luke's gospel and the book of Acts simply expand on how Jesus fulfilled this mission.[1]

This passage of Scripture is divided into two sections. First, Jesus was *anointed with the Holy Spirit* and power. God's Spirit gave Jesus, in His humanity, the power to heal the sick and cast out evil spirits. The Holy Spirit's power, God's power, was essential for His mission; without it nothing would happen. We, too, His followers, unless we are filled with the power of the Spirit, are like an automobile without a motor. The design, the exterior, may be beautiful, but without the motor nothing moves.

Second, the Spirit then enabled Jesus to fulfill *His basic mission*:

- to preach Good News to the poor (that is, blessings are free for those who cannot pay for them)
- to give liberty to captives (that is, deliverance from evil)
- to give the blind new sight (that is, physical and spiritual healing)
- and to proclaim the Lord's year of favor (that is, the Year of Jubilee when debts—sins—are to be forgiven)

This is the very heart of the Gospel, and when Jesus later shared His own mission with the Twelve, we see exactly the same pattern. First of all, He gave His followers a share in His own divine power and authority: "He called his twelve disciples to him and gave them authority to drive out evil spirits and to heal every disease and sickness" (Matthew 10:1; see also Luke 9:1).

Then, after that, they were empowered as He had been to share His own healing mission: "As you go, proclaim that the kingdom of heaven is close at hand. Cure the sick, raise the dead, cleanse the lepers, cast out devils" (Matthew 10:7–8, JB).

Over the centuries, preachers and theologians increasingly spiritualized these extraordinary statements. For example, "to give the blind new sight" came to mean that God opens our spiritual eyes so we can recognize the truth of Christian preaching. Having our spiritual eyes opened is a marvelous gift, of course, but Jesus meant more than that; He promised to heal the physically blind as well. He made this clear when John the Baptist (who was locked up in Herod's prison) sent two of his disciples to ask Jesus whether or not He was "the one to come." When John's messengers arrived, Jesus was busy curing many people of bodily diseases and casting out evil spirits, and so He instructed the messengers to

"Go back and report to John what you have seen and heard: The blind receive sight, the lame walk, those who have leprosy are cured, the deaf hear, the dead are raised, and the good news is preached to the poor. Blessed is the man who does not fall away on account of me."

Luke 7:22–23

In other words, Jesus was demonstrating that He was the long-awaited Messiah precisely because He healed the physically sick. Matthew made the very same point in his gospel, first by describing how Jesus healed three physical sicknesses, including leprosy and a fever, and then summing it all up:

When evening came, many who were demon-possessed were brought to him, and he drove out the spirits with a word and healed all the sick. This was to fulfill what was spoken through the prophet Isaiah: "He took up our infirmities and carried our diseases."

Matthew 8:16–17

This was the Good News, the basic Christian proclamation. It is News because it is happening now; it is Good because the evil that has weighed upon the human race is at last being lifted off.

The teachings in the gospel consist not only of what Jesus said but also of what He *did*. Over and over the gospels talk about what Jesus "did and said." Jesus not only talked about healing and liberation, He did it. He healed and cast out evil spirits. The history of the early

Church is not called "The Sayings of the Apostles" but "The *Acts* of the Apostles."

Jesus' Priorities

And now, consider how Jesus arranged the priorities in His life. If we were in His situation and realized that we had only three years to accomplish our mission, do you think we might have tried to come up with a better, more efficient plan than His? I mean, why spend so much time laying hands on crowds of sick people? Why not spend that time preparing talks and writing training manuals? A secretary could help organize the pertinent ideas for key subjects, such as war and peace and how to reconcile conflicted families. Aren't all these crowds of sick people a huge distraction from the really important work of teaching?

My response is that if we really imitate Christ, we will be followed by crowds of sick people and not just the well-to-do of the social set.

Undoubtedly Jesus thought about all that, but in spite of the seeming "inefficiency" He expended most of His energy healing the sick and casting out evil spirits. And not only did these individuals take Him away from "more important" tasks, most of them could not help Him out, either through their political influence or by donating money. In fact, He told some of the people He healed to keep quiet about it and not to broadcast the news. He wasn't looking for fame, nor was He out to prove something. Aware of His compassion and desire to heal, crowds hounded Him and prevented Him from moving around freely. When He wanted to rest, He had to take His disciples and retreat to Gentile territory, to places like Tyre and Sidon (in today's Lebanon), where no one would speak to Him, a Jew. He went where the Arabs lived.

Not only did His unscheduled life take valuable time away from His teaching, but it seems there might be more efficient methods of praying for the sick. Why not, for example, do what healing evangelists do today: Gather everyone together and pray for all of them all at once? Hold a one-hour healing service instead of exhausting yourself by dealing with human need from dawn to sunset. That makes sense, doesn't it?

And yet He spent His time and energy helping the sick and oppressed one at a time. He talked with them. After touching a blind man, He asked him, "Can you see anything?" And when He found out the man wasn't able to see clearly yet, but that people looked blurred, like trees walking around, He reached out and touched him a second time. At last the blind man saw clearly (see Mark 8:22–26). If you were Jesus' manager, wouldn't you have encouraged Him to set better priorities? After all, if you have only three years (or perhaps it was closer to two) to change the entire world, every minute counts. How could Jesus justify wasting so much time with these needy individuals while a whole suffering world waited for His profound teaching?

Clearly Jesus saw His priorities in a different light than most of us do today, and He made a decision. His priority, when He was not teaching, was to spend most of His time healing the sick and casting out evil spirits. And His preference was to spend time with the poor and the outcasts of society who could not repay Him.

Anyone who has been involved in a healing ministry has likely heard comments like this: "I know a wealthy man who is terminally ill and he wants you to come to his home and pray for him. Then, if he gets healed he might fund your ministry for years to come." This is the way people ordinarily think, but the potential for personal gain did not seem to affect Jesus at all. He had no hidden agenda in healing the sick. They were simply God's children. When Jesus was told that Herod was out to kill him, He responded, "You may go and give that fox this message: Look! Today and tomorrow I drive out devils and heal, and on the third day I attain my end. But for today and tomorrow and the next day I must go on" (Luke 13:32–33, NJB). That was Jesus' own view of what He did day by day: "I drive out devils and I heal the sick." Does that one line describe the everyday schedules of Christian leaders in our day—"I drive out devils and heal the sick"?

Healing was so clearly at the center of Jesus' mission that the only way to escape it is to deny that the miracles really happened and to claim that they are fanciful legends. There is no other option: In the gospels "signs and wonders" are at the center of the story.

As N. T. Wright explains:

Jesus *did* things and then commented on them, explained them, challenged people to figure out what they meant. He acted practically and symbolically, not least through his remarkable works of healing—works that today all but the most extreme skeptics are forced to regard as in principle historical. . . . Jesus soon became better known for healing than baptizing. And it was his remarkable healings, almost certainly, that won him a hearing. He was not a teacher who also healed; he was a prophet of the kingdom, first enacting and then explaining that kingdom. I take the healings as read, then, and move on at once to the explanations.[2]

This was the witness of those who walked with Jesus as well. When Peter was called to the home of Cornelius and met with the first group of Gentiles who were to become followers of Jesus, he summed up the entire three-year ministry of Jesus by telling them

"how God anointed Jesus of Nazareth with the Holy Spirit and power, and how he went around doing good and healing all who were under the power of the devil, because God was with him."

Acts 10:38

Again, it goes back to Jesus' inaugural address and His vision. He was empowered by the Holy Spirit, and this enabled Him to overcome the evil that weighs upon the human race by healing everyone who is under the power of Satan.

Jesus' Passion

Not only did Jesus spend extraordinary amounts of time fulfilling His mission—praying for those who were suffering, including the poor and disenfranchised—but He did so fearlessly, moving in ways that were guaranteed to create opposition. The most notable was His healing people on the Sabbath. He openly broke the law of the Sabbath, as the religious leaders of His day understood its correct observance, and they hated Him for it.

Take, for example, the way that He healed the crippled woman who had been bent over for eighteen years (see Luke 13:10–17). How easy it would have been for Him to heal her privately! Instead, He stood her up in the middle of the synagogue. Then He laid His hands on her and at last she was free.

And if He wanted to heal her publicly, why didn't He wait one more day until the Sabbath was over? After all, she had been that way for years and years, and her arthritis wasn't life threatening. Why risk His life? If He had asked her if she minded waiting another day, she probably would have said, "I don't want You to get killed over this. It's not worth it! I'll be glad to wait until tomorrow." That is what the irate synagogue official claimed that He should have done: "There are six days for work. So come and be healed on those days, not on the Sabbath" (Luke 13:14). Ordinary people rejoiced when they saw healing take place, but the religious leaders were furious.

Since people are no longer killed for breaking the Sabbath, it is hard for us to imagine what this experience must have been like for Jesus. Basically, He was not just getting into a verbal argument with the synagogue leaders; He was throwing a public challenge in their faces.

And He did it more than once.

Along with the woman set free after eighteen years of suffering, the gospels describe four other individuals whom Jesus healed on the Sabbath:

- the man with the withered hand (see Matthew 12:9–14; Mark 3:1–6; Luke 6:6–11)
- the man with dropsy healed in a Pharisee's house (see Luke 14:1–6)
- the lame man at the pool of Bethesda (see John 5:1–18)
- the man born blind (see John 9:1–41)

So often did He heal on the Sabbath that the religious leaders openly talked about killing Him. When Jesus heard about these plots, He responded, "Why are you angry with me for making a man whole and complete on a sabbath?" (John 7:23, JB).

William Barclay writes about how hard it is for us to understand Jesus' revolutionary decision unless we first understand the utmost seriousness with which the religious leaders regarded the correct way of keeping the Sabbath. "The Law forbade all work on the Sabbath day, and so the orthodox Jews would literally die rather than break it."[3] During the uprising of the great Jewish leader, Judas Maccabaeus, for instance, his followers were trapped in caves by the Greek general Antiochus. On the Sabbath the Greek army attacked the Jewish soldiers, who were all massacred when they refused to fight on the holy day. As a result, one thousand Jews—men, women and children—were killed, because they refused to take up arms on the Sabbath.[4]

The most famous story encouraging zeal for the Law's strict observance tells about seven brothers who heroically suffered torture and death—while their mother watched them die—rather than eat pork.

> The king tried to force them to taste pig's flesh, which the Law forbids, by torturing them with whips and scourges. One of them, acting as spokesman for the others, said, "What are you trying to find out from us? We are prepared to die rather than break the laws of our ancestors."
>
> The king, in a fury, ordered pans and cauldrons to be heated over a fire. As soon as they were red-hot he commanded that this spokesman of theirs should have his tongue cut out, his head scalped and his extremities cut off, while the other brothers and his mother looked on. When he had been rendered completely helpless, the king gave orders for him to be brought, still breathing, to the fire and fried alive in a pan.[5]

These religious leaders who opposed Jesus were not wicked, prejudiced officials; they were dedicated to keeping the Sabbath, as they understood it. They were ready to die in defense of their law, in contrast to Jesus, who was ready to die to break that very same law!

For Jesus even to have stood up and questioned their interpretation of the Sabbath law invited them to kill Him. But to go beyond talk and actually do it—to stand someone up in public and then perform a healing—shows us Jesus' remarkable determination. It is a teaching in itself.

But consider this: Jesus did not have to risk His life by healing publicly on the Sabbath. Why was healing so important to Jesus that He was willing to risk death?

Healing was His passion.

When we realize that most Christians no longer feel that way, we have to ask ourselves what deep meaning Jesus saw in healing that fueled this extraordinary passion. The meaning is simply this: To Jesus, healing and deliverance were not merely "signs and wonders";

together with preaching, they were the central focus of His Kingdom message. The Messiah, the Savior, had come. Mankind's lost inheritance was about to be restored through His supreme sacrifice. "The Kingdom of God is at hand; the kingdom of evil is being destroyed" forms the basic teaching of Christianity. As John the Evangelist wrote, "The reason the Son of God appeared was to destroy the devil's work" (1 John 3:8).

In all of these confrontations we cannot miss seeing Jesus' fierce determination to heal the sick. If we think about it, it is truly extraordinary, His strength and boldness, His sureness about being right.

And what is He right about? John's gospel quotes Jesus as saying that He did only what He saw His Father doing (see John 5:19–20). This suggests that Jesus considered the leaders' interpretation of the Law to be wrong—and not only wrong but absolutely destructive. Their interpretation was so wrong, in fact, that Jesus considered it a matter of life and death that it be changed.

Jesus loved His Father's Law, and He was showing us that human interpretations of it have falsified its purpose. The Father's main concern is bringing life and health to His children. The Sabbath was made for human beings, not human beings for the Sabbath. Jesus would not join in their pretense of honoring God while letting people suffer needlessly because of their legalistic interpretation of some law that originally was meant to honor God.

Why did Jesus risk death? Because healing was a life and death issue. He was zealous to let people know what kind of a God His Abba was, one who desires mercy, not sacrifice (see Matthew 9:13). The healing ministry is intimately connected with the life, suffering, death and resurrection of Jesus. "By his wounds we are healed" (Isaiah 53:5).

I am writing this during the week before Easter when Christians are reflecting on the crucifixion and death of Jesus. The "official" reason given for condemning Jesus at His trial was that He claimed to be a king whose Kingdom threatened the Roman emperor's rule, but even Pilate found no subversion in Him (see Luke 23:1–4). Rather, it is most probable that the primary reason Jesus was arrested was because He broke the Law by healing on the Sabbath. It is true to say that He died for our sins, but it is also true to say that He died to heal the sick.

In fact, the first attempt to kill Jesus happened when He pointed out that God healed Arabs like Naaman, the Syrian general.

All the people in the synagogue were furious when they heard this. They got up, drove him out of the town, and took him to the brow of the hill on which the town was built, in order to throw him down the cliff.

Luke 4:28–29

This happened immediately after the same crowd was amazed and delighted at His inaugural address, in which He talked about His great mission to heal and liberate. But when He started talking about healing Gentiles, that put Him outside their understanding of God's love and His Law.

For us, the challenge becomes whether or not we will take healing as seriously as He did. Are we as passionate as Jesus was—as compassionate as Jesus was—and is?

Since Christian lives are meant to be modeled after Jesus' character ("What would Jesus do?"), it becomes obvious that we, too, should share His intense desire to heal the sick. Will we be like Him? Or will we be like the ones Paul described: "They will keep up the outward appearance of religion but will have rejected the inner power of it" (2 Timothy 3:5, JB)?

6

BASIC CHRISTIAN PREACHING

Jesus' great mission was to proclaim that the Kingdom of God is now present among us. And that being the case, the work of restoration can begin. Healing and exorcism, along with the need for Holy Spirit empowerment, are, therefore, essential to the Gospel message.

"The Kingdom of God Is at Hand"

Most Scripture scholars agree upon one thing: Jesus centered His teaching on proclaiming that "the Kingdom of God is at hand." This was the Good News, the Gospel. The phrase sounds majestic, uplifting, but what does it really mean to us today, in our own words? What do we think really happens when the Kingdom of God is in our midst? If we ask ordinary churchgoers on Sunday morning what it means to say that the Kingdom of God is already here in our midst, how do you think they would answer?

Most would probably say that the Kingdom of God is "heaven," a place where they hope to go in the future when they die. And while heaven is a wonderful part of God's Kingdom, scholars conclude that Jesus was not just talking about a place or time we will experience in the future. Jesus was talking about the present—about *now*.[1] "The Kingdom of God is at hand; it's in your midst" is the way He put it. It is true that we will not experience the fullness of that Kingdom until after we die, when God "will wipe away every tear," but Jesus preached that God's Kingdom is present among us even now.

Even the phrase *kingdom of heaven*, which we read in Matthew's gospel (as compared to *kingdom of God*, which we find in Mark and Luke), does not refer only to a place called "heaven," where God's people will go after death. Instead, it means a time when the rule of heaven—that is, the rule of God, the Kingdom of God—is brought to bear upon the present world. Jesus taught us to pray, "Thy kingdom come, Thy will be done *on earth* as it is in heaven."

This is key, because so many Christians think that this life on earth is simply a testing time, a trial to be endured. As I mentioned in chapter 1, many people believe that if they endure suffering in this life with courage and faith, they will be rewarded in the next life. Although this is certainly true, we are nevertheless meant to experience the first fruits of heaven, the down payment of heaven, even in this earthly life. You may have heard the phrase "All the way to heaven is heaven." Anything less is missing the mark. It was, for instance, the prevalent Christian belief that the Kingdom of heaven is all in the future that enabled the Communists to claim that religion was nothing more than the opium of the people. When we deny that God's Kingdom breaks into our lives here and now to liberate us, we buy into a lie that weakens the healing ministry.

As Jesus and the early Christians saw it, a whole new creation was breaking in upon them—a new life, an exciting life. Paul is practically shouting in his epistles, he is so excited: "If anyone is in Christ, he is a new creation; the old has gone, the new has come!" (2 Corinthians 5:17).

This beautiful new creation is the heart of the Christian message: the Kingdom of God is breaking in all around us!

The Other Side of the Good News

What good news! As the Kingdom of God comes in, the evil that has weighed us down is at last being lifted off.

There is no denying that we face great obstacles to growing in our new life, once we have been born into it. We are bombarded constantly by the forces of sickness and death. For us to grow in the love of God and the love of our fellow human beings, we need to be freed of all those evils that prevent us from experiencing the kind of vibrant life that God intends for us. Without the Holy Spirit's ability to overcome Satan and the powers of sickness—mental, moral, physical—we are blocked from experiencing the fullness of new life that Jesus came to give us. For this reason, in addition to saying, "The Kingdom of God is at hand," we also need to proclaim, "The kingdom of Satan is being destroyed!" That is the other side of the Good News!

And that is why, when Jesus sent His disciples out to preach about God's Kingdom, He also gave them the twin commissions of healing the sick and casting out evil spirits. It all fits together. In fact, unless Jesus had the power to destroy the evil that weighs upon us all, He could hardly say, "The Kingdom of God is here; the kingdom of Satan is being destroyed." Without the power of the Spirit to make it all come true, our preaching tends to be just a pious abstraction ("pie in the sky," as the Marxists claimed).

In the first chapter of Mark, we read how Jesus met a man who was possessed with an unclean spirit that cried out, "What do you want with us, Jesus of Nazareth? Have you come to destroy us?" The implied answer to this, of course, is "Yes, I have come to destroy you," and Jesus proceeded to cast out the unclean spirit, who departed with a loud shriek.

The people's response is instructive: They were amazed and asked what it all meant. Then they immediately answered their own question: "A new teaching—and with authority! He even gives orders to evil spirits and they obey him" (Mark 1:27). They saw right away that the exorcism was not just a spectacular event, a "sign and wonder." Underlying the dramatics, there was a profound, new teaching: The power of Satan over the human race was finally being challenged and destroyed. Humankind would at last be able to reclaim its lost inheritance.

Most of the rest of Mark's first chapter is devoted to Jesus' healing people, beginning with His healing Peter's mother-in-law of a fever. The response of the sick and oppressed was immediate. They sought their freedom and chased after Jesus. Already, before the first chapter of Mark is finished, we see Jesus having to escape the enthusiastic crowds. Without telling even Peter where He was going, He got up long before dawn to get away from the crowd so He could speak to people in other towns (see Mark 1:35–39).

You may notice that writers and teachers often portray these healings as side issues, miraculous enticements to hear His teachings, *but the healings and exorcisms were part of the teaching itself.* They were why Jesus came. They were His mission. They are why we call Him by His main title, "our Savior."

As we have said, His very name, *Jesus*, tells us His mission: "God heals; God saves."

Unless we share in Jesus' ministry of healing the sick and casting out evil spirits, our preaching about the Kingdom of God being here among us is simply an empty promise.

Jesus' teaching was demonstrated by His action: He had the authority to back it up. This is the basic teaching of the Gospel, which we have largely lost: The Kingdom of God is here; the kingdom of Satan is being destroyed.

If we are going to preach as Jesus preached, then, we also have to receive the gift of healing the sick and casting out evil spirits. This is not to say that everyone we pray for will be physically healed, but healing should happen often enough so that we can see the Kingdom of God breaking in among us, even now.

Now let's explore the work in our lives of the One who makes the Kingdom of God come to earth: the Holy Spirit.

7

THE BAPTISM
WITH THE HOLY SPIRIT

As we said in discussing Jesus' inaugural address (see Luke 4:16–28), He made two claims about His life: (1) He was anointed with the power of God's Spirit, and (2) this gave Him the ability to proclaim liberty to captives and to heal the sick.

Jesus, in His humanity, needed at some point in His life to experience the baptism with the Holy Spirit. As you know, for three hundred years Christian leaders tried to understand how Jesus could be both human and divine. They finally concluded that He was one person, the second Person of the Trinity, but He had two natures: He was fully divine and fully human.

It is all a mystery, but as a human being He went through the growth that we all go through as human beings: "And Jesus grew in wisdom and stature, and in favor with God and men" (Luke 2:52). As an example of ancient Christian tradition, Philoxenus (ca. 440–523) believed that up to the time of His baptism in the Jordan, Jesus still lived under the Law.[1] After that He was led by the Holy Spirit and His teaching had the authority of God behind it.

For us it is significant that Jesus needed to be baptized by the Spirit precisely because He was a human being like us. It means that He is, therefore, the model for every Christian's walk. The very term *Christian* indicates that we should be like Christ—"anointed" with the Spirit and continuing His ministry. This is not just a spiritual or poetic way of talking about a great idea: The power is real, and the healings are real.

When we claim to be Christians, are we saying only that we believe certain doctrines? Or are we also saying, "Just as Jesus was the Christ because He was filled with the Holy Spirit, I, too, am filled with Christ's Spirit. That's what makes me fully Christian"?

Jesus' Own Baptism with the Spirit

Let's look at Jesus' baptism more closely, as told in the gospel of Mark. Before He could begin His public ministry, Jesus needed to receive His own personal baptism by water and the Spirit.

Mark begins by describing how John the Baptist prepared the way for Jesus, prophesying that Jesus would be the one who would baptize His people in the Holy Spirit—His main mission as Messiah (see Mark 1:7–8).

Mark then tells how Jesus went to John the Baptist at the Jordan River and asked to be baptized. After Jesus came up out of the water, the Spirit appeared in the form of a dove. As Luke makes clear, Jesus' baptism in the Spirit happened when Jesus was praying *after* John's water baptism, not as a result of it. "Heaven opened and the Holy Spirit descended on him in bodily shape, like a dove. And a voice came from heaven, 'You are my Son, the Beloved; my favor rests on you'" (Luke 3:22, JB). [2]

The Holy Spirit then "drove" Jesus into the wilderness to confront Satan, the very root of evil in this world (see Mark 1:12–13). Jesus overcame the ultimate enemy, the source of human misery, and then traveled on into Galilee, "proclaiming the good news of God. 'The time has come,' he said. 'The kingdom of God is near. Repent and believe the good news!'"(Mark 1:14–15).

Then Jesus moves out and starts to free, one by one, those unhappy individuals who had been under Satan's dominion.

We are still in the first chapter of Mark when we read about His encounter with a demoniac, described earlier, after which the people marvel at the "new teaching." And what is the new teaching? It is simply that Jesus has the authority to give orders to evil spirits, who obey Him. In other words, here is a man who has God's own power, the power of the Spirit to overcome the evil that weighs upon the human race.

From that point on, Jesus cast out evil spirits wherever He encountered them and healed the sick whenever they asked for help. We get some idea of the scope of this ministry by looking at the passages that mark transitions between different sections of the gospels. These transitions are summaries of large numbers of healings and exorcisms. Matthew, for example, includes five of these passages (see Matthew 4:23–25; 8:16–17; 9:35; 14:34–36; 15:29–31). Here is a typical healing transition:

> Jesus went throughout Galilee, teaching in their synagogues, preaching the good news of the kingdom, and healing every disease and sickness among the people. News about him spread all over Syria, and people brought to him all who were ill with various diseases, those suffering severe pain, the demon-possessed, those having seizures, and the paralyzed, and he healed them. Large crowds from Galilee, the Decapolis, Jerusalem, Judea and the region across the Jordan followed him.
>
> Matthew 4:23–25

Truly, He is the Christ, the Man anointed with God's power to rescue our wounded humanity! And He expects us to follow not only His teaching, but His example.

Why Do We Need to Be Baptized with the Spirit?

We do not often consider that heresy exists in some of our churches today, but it does and it is this: We consider Jesus only as the teacher of a great ideal. He was, of course, a magnificent teacher of the greatest message the world will ever hear. But, as we have said, He is also our Savior, our Redeemer. This means that, in addition to His ability to teach a great ideal, He enables, empowers us to live that ideal, which is well beyond our own abilities. He not only saves us from our sins but shares with us the Holy Spirit, whose *power* transforms our lives. And He is also our example. This means that we are meant to reach out, in the power of the Spirit, to heal and transform a wounded humanity.

The coming of the Spirit is the *great promise* proclaimed by Jesus' precursor, John the Baptist. As we all know, John the Baptist was the great prophet who came to prepare the way of the Lord. The Baptist's only prophecy about Jesus that is found in all four gospels is that He is the one who will baptize us with the Holy Spirit (Matthew and Luke add "and with fire"). In the Baptist's words, Jesus' main mission is to baptize us in the Spirit. Is this taught in most of our churches? And what does it mean?

Literally, the meaning of baptism is that Jesus will "immerse" us in the Holy Spirit. In the practical world, it means that the Holy Spirit is the one who will empower us and change us into a new creation, a new kind of humanity. The Spirit is also the one who will give us all the supernatural charisms we need to carry on His mission in our day. In other words, baptism with the Spirit is the means by which we follow Jesus' example of proclaiming the Kingdom and reaching out to a hurting world.

So often the Twelve are seen as extraordinary—a special class of people who are represented today by another special class, the clergy. That is why it is important to remember another group of followers: When Jesus chose 72 nameless disciples to go out and minister in His name, He made it clear that He empowers and ennobles ordinary people. Like the Twelve, the "ordinary" 72 came back rejoicing because they were successful; they were amazed because they had actually seen demons cast out. And Jesus Himself rejoiced because God had shown all these marvels to the simple and humble, revealing them "to little children" and hiding them from the learned and clever (see Luke 10:17–21).

And we don't even know the names of these 72!

When Jesus empowered the 72 disciples to help Him preach and heal, it reflected the time when a desperate, disheartened Moses complained to God that the people were overwhelming him with their needs. Moses cried out:

"Where can I get meat for all these people? They keep wailing to me, 'Give us meat to eat!' I cannot carry all these people by myself; the burden is too heavy for me. If this is how you are going to treat me, put me to death right now—if I have found favor in your eyes—and do not let me face my own ruin."

Numbers 11:13–15

Instead of being angry at Moses' despairing lament, God answered Moses' prayer (if that's what it is) by telling him to select seventy men whom he knew to be leaders and to tell them to go to the Tent of Meeting. There, God would take some of the Spirit that was on Moses and place it on them. After this empowerment they could help Moses carry the burden of the people so he would not have to bear it alone (see Numbers 11:16–17).

The Lord then came down in the cloud to speak with Moses and put the Spirit on the seventy elders. And "when the Spirit rested on them, they prophesied, but they did not do so again" (Numbers 11:25). The Spirit even came down on two men, Eldad and Medad, who had not come to the Tent of Meeting and they also prophesied. A jealous Joshua complained about this to Moses, who retorted, "I wish that all the LORD's people were prophets and that the LORD would put his Spirit on them!" (Numbers 11:29).

This was a foreshadowing of Pentecost. It was also clearly a foreshadowing of Jesus calling the 72 in a mini-Pentecost, but it was

- partial: only some of God's Spirit was placed on Jesus' followers
- temporary: it lasted only for a certain time

This partial sharing also foreshadowed the outpouring of God's Holy Spirit on everyone who is open to it.

Just as the early followers of Jesus carried on His mission by healing the sick, they also understood that they could not fulfill their mission unless they received the power of the Spirit.

What Is the Baptism with the Holy Spirit?

The New Testament nowhere gives a definition of the baptism with the Spirit, but it does describe what the baptism does. We have already spoken about receiving the *power* of Christ, especially the power to heal and cast out evil spirits. I have prayed for hundreds—maybe thousands—of people to receive it; perhaps these insights from that ministry will help us understand its further purpose.

First, the word *baptism* means "immersion," so Spirit baptism is like being immersed in water. It is, in fact, generally connected with water baptism, especially when it is by immersion. In the early Church, adults who were baptized expected, at the same time, to be baptized in the Spirit; they regarded the two experiences as the same event.

Second, Jesus considered it to be of *supreme importance*. The Church in its fullness was not born until the people were filled with the Spirit. It was not something you achieved but it was something that God did for you; remember that the apostles and disciples had to wait until it happened at Pentecost. It was pure gift.

Third, baptism with the Spirit is usually accompanied by *external signs*. Emotionally, it usually leads to an overflow of great joy. Spiritually, some of the charismatic gifts—especially praying in tongues—usually accompany it. Peter's sermon in the household of Cornelius was interrupted by an explosion of tongues (see Acts 10:46).

Fourth, different parts of our being are touched by the Spirit:

- Our *minds* are enlightened. People who once felt that reading Scripture was a chore now find delight in reading it. Passages that once seemed dense now open up (see John 14:26).
- We often receive *guidance* about what to do or not to do (see John 16:13).
- We will notice a change within our *spirit*: the Father, Son and Holy Spirit will come and live within us, and we will know and love them in a deeper way. Jesus will love us and show Himself to us (see John 14:21).
- We shall be *protected* from the evil one (see John 17:15).
- Jesus' love, joy and peace shall be within us (see John 14:27; 15:9, 11).

Many other things have taken place after people have received the baptism with the Spirit. Some of my friends have been healed of long-standing addictions and problems in their relationships, and some of their financial burdens have been lifted. I just today received a letter that reads in part: "Words truly cannot express the gratitude I feel for your being a conduit for God's blessing and anointing as you prayed for our individual healing, as well as for us to receive the baptism of the Holy Spirit. I'm still processing all that has happened, and more is happening by the day. I can only tell you this for sure—our lives will never be the same!"

There is no one list of things that always happens to every person. It is as if God tailors the outpouring of the Spirit to each person individually.

For those baptized as infants, the Spirit's indwelling cannot manifest itself in the same way as for adults. In some cases it appears that the Spirit's influence gradually grows in us as we ourselves grow physically. I believe that is the way it often happens. Usually these individuals can remember no specific time when some great spiritual event took place in their lives; God's presence was always there.

For others of us, the encounter with the Spirit is dramatic and sudden, usually coming during a prayer to receive the Spirit—or to receive the fullness of the Spirit for those who already have the Spirit to some degree (as the apostles did before Pentecost). It involves a release of the gifts of the Spirit, which have been bound up before.

My friend the late Reverend Tommy Tyson defined the baptism with the Spirit as an "event in our lives through which we become more continually aware of the presence, the person and the power of the risen Christ." These words and phrases are packed with meaning. *More continually aware* indicates that the person before the Spirit baptism may have already been aware of Christ's presence. Others seem to receive the power of the Spirit for the first time.

The baptism brings a great increase in this awareness. When priests or ministers are baptized in the Spirit, their preaching often changes and becomes more personal. And people notice it. Once when I prayed for a priest in Peru, his preaching changed so dramatically that six of the people in his church got on a bus and rode overnight to hear our team speak about the Spirit in the town of Chimbote.

The *risen* Christ becomes more real as well. Many Christians concentrate on the suffering, crucified Christ but have little experience of the risen Christ. If you travel to Latin America and look at the religious art, you are immediately made aware of the concentration there on suffering and death. Paintings and statues of Jesus usually either show Him as an infant at His mother Mary's breast, or as an adult suffering in agony on the cross. What is mostly absent is an adult, healthy Jesus, as He is now, to whom we can relate as Lord, as brother and as friend.

From having seen what happens to the people I know who have experienced the baptism with the Holy Spirit, I can only say that it is often a truly transforming event. No wonder Jesus told His followers that they were not to leave Jerusalem until they received it. As Luke recorded it, these were Jesus' last words on earth: "Stay in the city until you have been clothed with power from on high" (Luke 24:49).

How the Spirit Changes Our Lives

Over the centuries some individuals and groups of Christians have rediscovered this spiritual power, notably in the past century. This is especially true of the Pentecostal churches, the charismatic groups in the mainline churches and now hosts of independent evangelical charismatics. In fact, those churches and groups that have experienced the power of the Spirit are growing at an extraordinary rate.[3] But most ordinary churchgoers remain unaware of their need for an explicit empowering of the Spirit in order to grow as Christians. Here are two important reasons to pray for this empowering.

1. We need the baptism *for our own personal growth*, to become the kind of new creation that St. Paul describes. Paul makes it clear that observing the Law will not achieve this: "What counts is a new creation" (Galatians 6:15). He talks about how the Holy Spirit transforms us through the fruits of the Spirit: "love, joy, peace, patience, kindness, goodness, faithfulness, gentleness and self-control" (Galatians 5:22–23).

Much of our preaching has to do with "sin management,"[4] but how many times do we hear that we need to pray for the transformation that can only be accomplished through the power of the Holy Spirit and not just through our own efforts? Without this hidden but real power, we cannot fulfill Christ's great commandment—loving as He loved, which is characterized by loving our enemies.

2. We also need to be empowered *to help other people*. This empowerment comes through all those charismatic gifts, mentioned by Paul in 1 Corinthians 12:4–11. These gifts include such charisms as healing, prophecy, discernment of spirits and the ability to interpret tongues. All these gifts are meant to help others. This is evident in the fact that the person who exercises them may or may not be holy. In regard to prophecy and casting out evil spirits, Jesus warned that some who have these gifts will be cast away at the Last Judgment:

> "Many will say to me on that day, 'Lord, Lord, did we not prophesy in your name, and in your name drive out demons and perform many miracles?' Then I will tell them plainly, 'I never knew you. *Away from me, you evil-doers!*'"
>
> Matthew 7:22–23, emphasis mine

These extraordinary gifts are meant to help others. On the other hand, for our own spiritual growth, we need to exhibit the fruits of the Spirit, those qualities that will help us become more like Christ. In my own experience, many people ask us to pray for them to receive the charismatic gifts, such as, "Please pray for me to receive the gift of healing." Relatively few ask for the fruits of the Spirit, saying something like, "I have trouble loving other people. Would you pray that I receive the gift of loving and caring?"

For all of this we need the power of God's Spirit.

Like Jesus' preaching, our own preaching should declare that the kingdom of Satan is being destroyed. That cannot happen by our own efforts. Only the power of God can heal the sick and free people from the evil that weighs them down on every level:

- We are distant from God and so we need the Spirit to help us come into an intimate *relationship with God*.
- Because we are burdened by sin, we need *forgiveness*.
- Some of us are infested or oppressed by evil spirits and need *deliverance*.

- Our bodies are sick; we need *physical healing.*
- Since we are ignorant and deluded, we need the *guidance* of the Holy Spirit.
- We are wounded emotionally and need emotional, *inner healing.*
- Our characters are flawed; we need to become like Christ through the *fruits of the Holy Spirit,* like love, joy and peace.

Unless all this healing and deliverance takes place (usually through prayer) we cannot realistically preach that the Kingdom of God is at hand and that the kingdom of Satan is being destroyed.

Without the power of God enabling this new creation to come into existence, we can only preach abstractions. We can only preach the Law.

That is why healing and deliverance are the two pillars of the Gospel: without them, people cannot change beyond a certain point. Like Paul we can only say, "I don't understand my own behavior. I don't do the things I want to do. Instead, I do the things I hate."

This is why it is tragic that the ministry of healing has died out. Without it, Christianity is sickly.

To resurrect the moribund, barely moving body of Christendom, we need to recover the three main promises of Jesus:

- a personal relationship with God through Jesus Christ
- our personal Pentecost, the baptism with the Spirit, the source of new life
- healing and liberation from all those forces that oppress us with evil—both spiritual and physical—and prevent us from experiencing God's vibrant life

To Sum Up

God had anointed him with the Holy Spirit and with power, and because God was with him,	Here is the source of Jesus' ministry and also of ours, the power of God's Spirit, which we receive in our personal Pentecost.
Jesus went about doing good and curing all who had fallen into the power of the devil (see Acts 10:38).	This is Jesus' mission, and ours, too: doing good by healing the sick and liberating people from the evil that oppresses them.

The basic heresy of the Church today is not doctrinal; we believe in the Holy Spirit and we may even celebrate the Feast of Pentecost. The problem lies in what we do—or rather, in what we fail to do.

Jesus was both human and divine, both man and God, and in His humanity He was empowered by the Holy Spirit to become the Anointed One, the Christ, in order to fulfill His healing mission. This should encourage us to imitate Him by being filled with the Spirit to carry on His ministry of healing.

8

MINISTRY WITH POWER

The News Spreads

One of the amazing things about Jesus' healing ministry is that He never tried to hold it to Himself, as if He were the only one who could heal the sick. He shared the ministry, first with the Twelve, then with the 72 and last with the entire Church. In the words of John Wimber, "Everyone gets to play!"

This is in stark contrast to our human tendency to narrow and limit this marvelous ministry—a sad process we shall describe later. Just to give you an idea of how exclusive it was, at one point, in the England of the 1520s, only *one person* held healing services: King Henry VIII.[1] Even clergymen did not pray for people to be healed. A hundred years later King Charles I even made it a crime for anyone else to pray for healing. The whole point was to show that the king was special—divinely anointed as no one else was. No one should dare rise up in revolt against him.

The Twelve Receive His Power

But back to Jesus. Matthew describes Jesus as making a tour of villages, preaching and healing the sick. But then He was overwhelmed at the sight of so many beaten-down people.

> When he saw the crowds, he had compassion on them, because they were harassed and helpless, like sheep without a shepherd. Then he said to his disciples, "The harvest is plentiful but the workers are few. Ask the Lord of the harvest, therefore, to send out workers into his harvest field."
>
> Matthew 9:36–38

Then Jesus answered His own prayer by choosing the Twelve and temporarily sharing with them His own power and authority. This enabled them to preach that the Kingdom of God was now in their midst, as well as to demonstrate it by healing and casting out evil spirits (see Matthew 10:1).

We notice at once this is not merely a technique He taught His followers about how to pray for the sick: God's power has to back up the prayer or it will not work.

The Seventy-Two Minister in Power

Later, we see that Jesus, finding that the multitudes of the sick could not be adequately helped by Himself alone or by the Twelve, decided to multiply those who shared His mission:

> After this the Lord appointed seventy-two others and sent them two by two ahead of him to every town and place where he was about to go. He told them, "The harvest is plentiful, but the workers are few. Ask the Lord of the harvest, therefore, to send out workers into his harvest field. . . . Heal the sick who are there and tell them, 'The kingdom of God is near you.'"
>
> Luke 10:1–2, 9

We have no idea who these 72 were; no names, just ordinary followers of Jesus. But we do know that they were excited about their mission when they came back. They found that it really worked. "The seventy-two returned with joy and said, 'Lord, even the demons submit to us in your name'" (Luke 10:17). Jesus then had to calm them down by reminding them that it was far more important that their names were written in heaven (see Luke 10:20).

One of the clearest teachings of the Gospel is that God chose the weak, by human standards, to demonstrate His power:

> But God chose the foolish things of the world to shame the wise; God chose the weak things of the world to shame the strong. He chose the lowly things of this world and the despised things—and the things that are not—to nullify the things that are.
>
> 1 Corinthians 1:27–28

Lest we think that we are not qualified even to consider being a part of this work, we should remember that in His humanity Jesus Himself did not have the proper qualifications to establish either His credibility or His mission:

- He was not a *priest* of the tribe of Levi, called to celebrate the religious rites of his people.
- Nor was He a *scribe*, who had gone through a formal study of Scripture in order to become a rabbi.
- Nor was He a *Pharisee*, part of the special group who sought moral perfection, not only by studying but by strictly observing the Law.
- Nor was He an *Essene*, one of that group of people who were so serious about separating themselves from a sinful world that they fled to the desert and formed a close-knit community, seeking moral purity and truth.
- Nor was He an appointed leader, an *elder* of the people.
- Moreover, He was from Galilee, a district of Israel looked down upon as being provincial and contaminated by Gentile influences. "Can anything good come out of Galilee?" was the normal response of respectable people. How could Jesus have anything to offer?

In short, Jesus had no credentials. "This is Joseph's son, surely?" was the skeptical comment of the people from his own hometown of Nazareth. Jesus was Everyman, like the Irish immigrants to New York in the 1800s, or the Hispanic migrant workers in our day.

In all of this we see God's design, to show us that God's strength is made manifest in our weakness: Jesus came from a poor family with no earthly power, no prestige, no wealth, and yet that was not a barrier to His fulfilling His mission. In fact, we may find that the lack of earthly powers or credentials, like our Master, is our best preparation for becoming ministers of spiritual power—of ministering healing and deliverance to God's people.

The Church Is Born

As we all remember, on Pentecost it happened. With a rush of wind and tongues of flame, everyone in the Upper Room—and later, thousands more—was filled with the Holy Spirit. They did not just accept a belief; they experienced a dramatic personal event, and then they spoke in tongues and prophesied. To everyone's amazement, they were understood by every ethnic group that was on pilgrimage to Jerusalem—Parthians, Medes and everyone else. So filled were they with joy that the bystanders accused them of being drunk. Peter's only defense for their enthusiastic behavior was that it was only nine o'clock in the morning, too early to be out drinking.

And this remarkable event was not just a one-time filling with the Spirit, as had been the case in Moses' day and even among Jesus' followers in His lifetime. It happened again, for instance, when the first Gentiles came to believe in Christ during Peter's reluctant visit to the home of Cornelius, the Roman centurion. This Gentile Pentecost was so noisy and dramatic it interrupted Peter's sermon! Everyone was astonished, "for they heard them speaking in tongues" (Acts 10:46).

Jesus' Great Promise

We need to recover a sense of how important this impartation of the Spirit was to Jesus and to the early Church.

We have described Jesus' passion to heal the sick, so it is not surprising to find that Jesus showed a similar passion for people to encounter the Holy Spirit. At one point He was planning on quietly going up to Jerusalem to attend the Feast of Tabernacles. Once He got there and saw the spiritual hunger of the desperate people, however, He could no longer keep silent, even though His enemies were on the lookout for a way to kill Him.

> Jesus stood and said in a loud voice, "If anyone is thirsty, let him come to me and drink. Whoever believes in me, as the Scripture has said, streams of living water will flow from within him." By this he meant the Spirit, whom those who believed in him were later to receive. Up to that time the Spirit had not been given, since Jesus had not yet been glorified.
>
> John 7:37–39

In Jesus' famous Last Discourse (see John 13–17), we find that His main promise was to send the Holy Spirit to His disciples—and to us. They were distraught because He was telling them that He had to go away and leave them. Since they were so worried Jesus tried to console them by explaining that it was actually better if He left them in His bodily presence. Unless He left, He could not come to them in a new way:

- "I will not leave you as orphans" (John 14:18).
- "Unless I go away, the Counselor [the Paraclete, the Comforter] will not come to you; but if I go, I will send him to you" (John 16:7).
- "On that day you will realize that I am in my Father, and you are in me, and I am in you" (John 14:20).

Jesus was promising that even though He was leaving in His physical presence, He would come and be with them (and us) in a new and much better way: He would come—with the Father and the Spirit—and live within us. That indwelling would be far better than having His physical presence still with us—but outside us—sitting down at a table to talk, walking the hillsides with us. (It is hard to believe that our situation today is actually better than if we were with Jesus two thousand years ago listening to Him on the Mount of Olives, but that's what He said.)

He also promised that when the Spirit comes to live within us we will be guided into all truth. "I have much more to say to you, more than you can now bear. But when he, the Spirit of truth, comes, he will guide you into all truth" (John 16:12–13). As my friend Tommy Tyson once said, "It's an inside job. God works now from the inside out, not from the outside in."

I encourage you to read once again Jesus' last instructions, given to His disciples on the night before He died (see John 14–17). Jesus ends this Last Discourse with a prayer to His Father, asking "that the love you have for me may be in them and that I myself may be in them" (John 17:26).

And the love with which the Father loved Jesus is the Holy Spirit—and Jesus prays that this deep, powerful love will be ours. If that were to happen in every heart, the human race would be transformed. War would cease.

After the Resurrection Jesus was again intent on one thing: that His disciples receive the Holy Spirit.

> On one occasion, while he was eating with them, he gave them this command: "Do not leave Jerusalem, but wait for the gift my Father promised, which you have heard me speak about. For John baptized with water, but in a few days you will be baptized with the Holy Spirit."
>
> Acts 1:4–5

Notice that Jesus went back to the beginning: He connected the sending of the Holy Spirit with the main prophecy of John the Baptist, that Jesus would be the one who would immerse them in the Holy Spirit. This was *the promise*.

In other words, the apostles were still not ready, even though

- they were His followers
- they knew Him
- they had listened to His teaching for several years
- they believed in the Resurrection

So they waited and prayed, and then, with a rush of wind and tongues of fire descending, all those in the Upper Room were filled with the Holy Spirit. And not only the one hundred and twenty, but three thousand others were filled that very day.

Let me stress again that this was not something they merely believed. They did believe, of course, and that is why they were willing to wait—for fifty days. But more than belief, something happened to them—God did something that transformed them.

It was visible; it was audible, as the *charisms* of the Spirit—tongues and prophecy—burst forth.

From this time on, the model for all of God's followers was that they

- be *filled with the Holy Spirit* (the Spirit baptism)
- be *empowered by the Spirit* with the *charisms* that would enable them to free and heal the suffering members of our human community

As Peter proclaimed on that buoyant day of Pentecost (quoting Joel 2:28–29):

> "In the last days, God says, I will pour out my Spirit on all people. Your sons and daughters will prophesy, your young men will see visions, your old men will dream dreams. Even on my servants, both men and women, I will pour out my Spirit in those days, and they will prophesy."
>
> Acts 2:17–18

The prophet Joel was here making a point that those groups in Israel that had the least status—women, slaves and young people—would all be equally blessed in this outpouring of the Spirit. Peter made sure there was no misunderstanding that every person was now a candidate for his or her own personal Pentecost: "The promise that was made is for you and your children, and for all *those who are far away, for all those whom the Lord* our God *will call to himself*" (Acts 2:39, JB, emphasis added).

Truly, "Everyone gets to play!"

What was missing up until the day of Pentecost? It was not new doctrines to believe. (Tommy Tyson taught that most Christians already know far more teaching than they live by.) It was an interior filling with the Holy Spirit, accompanied by a permanent empowering.

I once heard a Father Salvador Carillo address a group of priests in Mexico City. As I remember it, he said, "Don't worry too much about how to figure it all out theologically—the baptism in the Spirit and how it relates to the sacrament of confirmation. The question that you need to answer is: 'Has what happened to Peter at Pentecost happened to you?'"

That is the question to ask ourselves: "Has what happened to Peter—and everyone else—at Pentecost happened to me?"

Post-Pentecost Healing

The basic teaching of the book of Acts is that the early Christians simply carried on the work of Jesus by preaching that the Kingdom of God was at hand and then they made it all come true by healing the sick and casting out evil spirits.

It is significant that right after Pentecost (see Acts 2:1–41), the first major event that followed was a dramatic healing. When Peter and John were going up to the Temple to pray, a crippled beggar was carried past them—crippled from birth. He looked at them, hoping for a handout, but instead Peter and John said, "Look at us." Peter then told him:

> "Silver or gold I do not have, but what I have I give you. In the name of Jesus Christ of Nazareth, walk." Taking him by the right hand, he helped him up, and instantly the man's feet and ankles became strong. He jumped to his feet and began to walk. Then he went with them into the temple courts, walking and jumping, and praising God.
>
> Acts 3:6–8

The confidence and assurance shown by Peter and John are amazing. Someone has observed that Peter claimed that he had neither silver nor gold, but that he did have the power of Jesus to heal crippled limbs. Today the Church finds it difficult to make either of those two claims. Perhaps, too, there is a connection between the two: While today we certainly have silver and gold, with all the influence that comes from them, we no longer seem to have as much spiritual power to work miracles.

This dramatic healing led to the first persecution of Christians. It is significant that Peter and John were not arrested when they were preaching, just talking, but only after they healed the lame man. (How many religious leaders in recent centuries have been persecuted for healing the sick?) The Sanhedrin immediately ordered that Peter and John be arrested, because the healing attracted attention and led crowds of people to follow the apostles—the number of Christians quickly increased to five thousand. Here Luke makes a special point: The Sanhedrin "were astonished at the assurance shown by Peter and John, considering they were *uneducated laymen*" (Acts 4:13, JB, emphasis added).

We seem to have lost our assurance that, as followers of Jesus, perhaps we (like Peter) can offer the sick "what we have" and say, "In the name of Jesus Christ, walk." We may be tempted to avoid the challenge by saying, "Well, the disciples were a unique group specially chosen by Jesus to walk with Him. Peter and John were unusually gifted." And yet Luke emphasizes that in the eyes of the religious leaders of that day Peter and John were very ordinary. They were simple laymen, not priests in charge of official prayer; more than that, they were uneducated and, therefore, humanly unqualified.

And, besides, the book of Acts goes on to show that it was not just Peter and the other apostles who healed the sick; it was also Christians like Philip, who started out simply as one of seven men chosen to distribute food (see Acts 8).

And then came Paul, who also healed the sick and cast out demons. He represented the next generation, someone who had not walked with Jesus in His lifetime. In fact, Luke makes a special point of showing that Paul, who reached out to the Gentiles, performed the same kind of miracles as did Peter, the leader of the Hebrew believers.

| Raising the Dead: | Peter raises the woman Dorcas from the dead (see Acts 9:36–42). | Paul raises the young man Eutychus from the dead (see Acts 20:7–12). |

Healing Cripples:	Peter heals Aeneas who has been paralyzed for eight years (see Acts 9:32–35).	Paul heals a cripple in Lycaonia (see Acts 14:8–10).
Even Their Presence Heals:	Peter's shadow heals the sick who were laid out on sleeping mats in hopes that he might walk past (see Acts 5:15).	Bits of cloth touched by Paul cure the sick and even drive out evil spirits (see Acts 19:11–12).

Luke's parallels are no coincidence: He was a careful writer and here he simply showed that signs and wonders were an expected part of a Christian's life; we all are called to be part of Jesus' healing ministry.

Significantly, Luke did not write a definite, conclusive ending to the last chapter of Acts. He was indicating by this that our mission of announcing Good News and healing the sick will never come to an end:

Paul lived for two years in his rented house. He welcomed everyone who came to visit. He urgently presented all matters of the kingdom of God. He explained everything about Jesus Christ. His door was always open.

Acts 28:30–31, MESSAGE

This open ending indicates that the exciting mission of the Church was meant to continue on and on, and never finish until the end of time.

For three centuries, that is exactly what happened.

9

THE SPIRIT FLOURISHES

The First 325 Years

Spirit baptism, together with healing and exorcism, flourished in those early years following Pentecost. From those ancient times, long before the printing press, we have only a few records of how the poor, uneducated, ordinary Christians lived, but we have enough to know that they expected to be filled with and led by the Spirit.

Expectations of Spirit Baptism

Christians in the early Church believed that, when they prayed, the Spirit would show up accompanied by powerful manifestations. When Paul traveled to Ephesus, for example, he found a group of disciples who, to his surprise, had "not even heard that there is a Holy Spirit" (Acts 19:2). "When Paul placed his hands on them, the Holy Spirit came on them, and they spoke in tongues and prophesied. There were about twelve men in all" (Acts 19:6–7).

We noted in the last chapter that Gentiles in the household of Cornelius were filled with the Holy Spirit as Peter preached. He then gave orders for them to be baptized in water. Later, when Peter defended his actions before the skeptical leaders of the Jerusalem church, his proof that the Gentiles deserved water baptism was simply that the Spirit had fallen upon them—just as at Pentecost—and had inspired them to pray in tongues and to prophesy. Since God had just baptized them in the Spirit, who was he to deny them baptism in water?

Visible and audible signs of the Spirit's presence such as these were obviously important and this expectancy lasted for another three hundred years. In the third century, for example, when adults were baptized, it was expected that when they rose up out of the baptismal water, they might prophesy or start praying in tongues. (Infants were baptized during this time as well, but were not, of course, expected to show manifestations of the gifts. There was no subsequent confirmation, as baptism and confirmation were one ceremony.)

This connection in the early Church (up to the fourth century)—of receiving the baptism in the Spirit at the same time they received their water baptism—is a fascinating one. They were serious about it; in some places converts had to spend two or three years in preparation.

Part of that time was spent undergoing extensive teaching and not just one but many exorcisms. The Church knew by experience that pagan converts had attracted evil spirits simply by having lived in a pagan culture. Deacons performed these exorcisms for men and the deaconesses for women. A reminder of this practice still exists in the Roman Catholic baptismal rite where the priest is allowed to perform an exorcism, even though the candidate is an infant. The baby has not yet had a chance to commit a sin, but the practice follows the precautions of early Christians who believed that evil spirits might be picked up from a demonic environment.

During Lent the candidates for baptism presented themselves daily, not only to receive instruction but also to receive regular exorcisms to banish demons. Finally, on the morning of Holy Saturday the candidates came together for a most solemn session that consisted, in part, of a final formula of exorcism.[1]

Then on the vigil of Easter (or Pentecost) the candidates went to the place where the baptism was to occur, usually a large home where a baptismal pool had been built with three steps leading down and three other steps leading up. The men and women would enter this primitive baptistry separately and disrobe (they were used to doing this in the Roman baths). The deacon would immerse the men three times, baptizing them each time in the name of the Father and of the Son and of the Holy Spirit. Then separately a deaconess would perform the same ceremony for the women. As they came up out of the water they would dress in white robes. They trusted, in those early days, that the charisms would descend upon the candidates and that some of them would prophesy, pray in tongues or have a vision.

Then the door to the main part of the house would be opened and the bishop would be there to embrace the newly baptized and welcome them into the Christian community. After that they would celebrate the Lord's Supper for the first time and rejoice.

The Fathers of the early Church[2] all believed that the newly baptized should pray to receive the charisms. Tertullian, the most famous Christian writer of his day (ca. 160–225), addressed those preparing for baptism: "You blessed ones, for whom the grace of God is waiting, when you come up from the most sacred bath of the new birth, when you spread out your hands . . . ask your Father, ask your Lord, for the special gift of his inheritance, the distribution of charisms. . . ."[3] Cyril of Jerusalem (ca. 315–387) claimed that hermits, virgins and all the laity had charisms.[4]

Fathers Kilian McDonnell and George Montague did an extensive study on the relationship between water baptism and baptism in the Holy Spirit,[5] and they state that the early Church used the terms as if they were one and the same. They quote eleven early Christian authors, including St. Hilary of Poitiers and St. John Chrysostom, to show that these authorities expected that the charisms would be imparted when new Christians were baptized. McDonnell and Montague wrote their book hoping that baptism with the Spirit would once again become normative. "The recovery of the baptism in the Spirit and the charisms is needed in all the institutions of the church."[6]

My own belief is that confirmation or adult baptism is an ideal time to pray for what we call the baptism with the Holy Spirit.[7] I personally prayed for this empowerment in 1967 when several friends prayed that those gifts of the Spirit that were within me through baptism, confirmation and ordination might be fully released. (I relate this story in the appendix.) Before that date I had never asked God to heal the sick, nor had I ever asked God to free

anyone from the oppression of evil spirits. It was only after I received
the baptism in the Spirit that I first began to pray for healing and
deliverance.

Because I had never prayed for anyone's healing before that time
I can't compare before and after in my own experience, but I believe
that more people are healed after we receive the baptism with the Spirit
than before. Without the presence, the Person and the power of the
Holy Spirit at work in us, I don't believe that much will happen when
we pray for healing or try to cast out evil spirits. We are likely to face
the same obstacles that the itinerant exorcists, the sons of Sceva, faced.
When they tried to cast out evil spirits by pronouncing the name of
Jesus over the possessed, the demon responded: "Jesus I know, and
I know about Paul, but who are you?" (Acts 19:15). They knew the
right formula, the right words, but they did not have the power they
needed to drive out the evil spirits.

Healing and Deliverance Build the Church

Just as the early Church kept a lively practice of the baptism in the
Spirit, they also carried on Jesus' healing and deliverance ministries.

The reason why these ministries were so important to them is no
mystery. It goes back to the same reason that Jesus devoted so much
of His time and energy to healing the sick and casting out evil spirits:
It was a natural part of the incoming Kingdom of God. Jesus taught
His disciples to move in power to help spread the Good News until,
at Pentecost, the Church exploded with the fullness of the combined
ministry and message.

For the next three hundred years Christians were proud of their
healing mission and enthusiastically prayed for the sick and cast out
demons. Until Constantine was converted (A.D. 312) there were no
church buildings, and Christians simply met in their homes to worship. Since the vast majority of those early Christians could not read,
what they knew about their religion was what they learned in their
house churches. Moreover, the Church had not yet established which
books of the New Testament were inspired, and since the collections
of Scripture were written out by hand on calfskin and were costly and

rare, Christian leaders necessarily had to concentrate their teachings on a few central truths.[8]

Anyone Can Do It

Instead of urging caution and fear, leaders in the early Church encouraged everyone to become more active—to "Get out there and heal and cast out evil spirits." There was no special class of healers or exorcists. Women such as St. Eugenia (in the third century) were active in the ministry of casting out demons,[9] as were all members of the Church. Everybody still got to play.

In fact, the boasting of the early Christian writers was that God worked equally powerfully through the prayers of the lowliest members of society, not just the highest, to confound our human pride as well as to show His mercy. Arnobius (ca. 300), for example, stated that Jesus "chose fishermen, artisans, rustics, and unskilled persons of a similar kind, that they being sent through various nations, should perform all those miracles without any deceit and without any material aids. . . . By the application of His hand He removed the mark of leprosy. . . . Sores of immense size . . . He restrained from further feeding on the flesh, by the interposition of one word; and they, in like manner, compelled the obstinate and merciless cancer to confine itself to a scar."[10]

Church Father Origen (who was martyred ca. 253), noted that Christians cast out demons "merely by prayer and simple adjurations which the plainest person can use, because, for the most part, it is unlettered [illiterate] persons who perform this work." He added that exorcism does "not require the power and wisdom of those who are mighty in argument."[11] In other words, any Christian could do it.

Tertullian claimed that the *noblest* Christian life is "to exorcise evil spirits—to perform cures—to live to God."[12] He went so far as to try to convince pagans that they would get more real enjoyment in healing the sick and casting out evil spirits than by attending pagan plays and gladiatorial contests.[13] Can you imagine a pastor today in his Sunday morning sermon telling the men that they can have more fun driving out evil spirits on that afternoon than by watching NFL football?

The Message Hits Home

In a fascinating book titled *Christianizing the Roman Empire: A.D. 100–400,*[14] Dr. Ramsay MacMullen, a professor of history and classics at Yale University, reiterates that the first Christians were mostly an illiterate, uneducated group; very few were intellectuals or among the elite. Most of them came from the slave and worker caste that lived in squalid, crowded city quarters. Their religion was simple and, by the sophisticated standards of our time, might seem somewhat superstitious, but they strongly believed in the supernatural.[15]

For many pagans in their midst, this ability to address and overcome evil spirits was impressive. Justin Martyr, who wrote around A.D. 150, stated that Christians were able to drive out those demons that the pagans were helpless in casting out.[16] When the nonbelievers saw this manifest difference between themselves and these ordinary people, they were led, gradually, to conversion. As Jesus had promised, He had come to liberate the captives (see Luke 4:18). They were forced to admit, "Your God is stronger than ours."

Yet not all of their pagan neighbors were open to the freedom that was being offered, if it meant giving up their host of gods. In the bastion of Rome, for instance, the Roman Pantheon was dedicated to all the multitude of pagan gods. "Whatever works for you" was the general attitude.

These early Christians, however, based on the Jewish heritage of their beliefs, would not budge from the truth that there was only one God and that all the other gods were only idols or demons. Christians further claimed that religion, as the Romans practiced it, was idolatry and could not be tolerated. "Our God is the true God, and your god is no god at all."

Such a black-and-white attitude naturally resulted in conflict, and when Christians refused to offer sacrifice to the statue of the emperor, the "Divine Emperor," they were seen as revolting against the established political order and were sentenced to death. For the early Christians—as for the Jews—the First Commandment, "You shall not worship false gods," was the starting point of their religion. In this matter, they were not tolerant.

This intense opposition to committing idolatry by refusing to offer incense to the emperor or to a pagan god came at a price—often the

Christian's life. The fierce persecutions were not constant but depended on the emperor's priorities, but when the persecutions came they were extraordinarily cruel. Nero dipped the Christians in pitch and burned them to illuminate Rome. Saints Perpetua and Felicity, her servant, were torn by the beasts and St. Polycarp was burned to death. Peter was crucified upside down and Paul was beheaded in Rome. Martyrdom was the fate of most of the early popes. The Roman catacombs are filled with their tombs.

How the Truth Wins

Although they lived under the threat of being killed, these believers were still filled with zeal to convert their neighbors to the truth. Unlike our day, when an evangelist can preach freely, as Billy Graham once did to fifty thousand people in our giant Jacksonville football stadium, most evangelization took place in those early centuries one-on-one, face-to-face, in their own neighborhoods, in their own poor dwellings or at work.

We can picture the typical third-century village, much like the culture of the Middle East today, with simple people just trying to get enough to eat to stay alive, many people living in a single dwelling. As a Christian you hear that a neighbor's child is sick, so you quietly tell him that you believe that your God can heal the child. The family is desperate enough to test your God, so you come to their dwelling and tell them about the One God in whom you believe—and His Son, Jesus—who can heal the child. The parents say, "Yes, please pray." So you do. And the child is healed.

Word travels fast, and others want you to tell them about this Jesus. One by one, family by family, it happens. They declare their allegiance to the one true God and receive further teaching, more in-depth, about Christianity. And eventually you hope they will ask for baptism.

Even under the threat of death they continued to proclaim the Kingdom of God and to show demonstrations of God's power—and they had many opportunities to do so. In the early Church—as in the Third World today—people not only believed in evil spirits but actively experienced demonic power firsthand. To proclaim the Kingdom of God was not just to get into a persuasive argument about the truth of Christianity; it meant casting out evil spirits and demonstrating God's power. As Paul claimed:

> I came among you in weakness, in fear and great trembling and what I spoke and proclaimed was not meant to convince by philosophical argument, but to demonstrate the convincing power of the Spirit, so that your faith should depend not on human wisdom but on the power of God.
>
> 1 Corinthians 2:3–4, NJB

As late as the thirteenth century Thomas Aquinas[17] explained this passage as meaning that Paul confirmed the truth of his teaching by the power of the Holy Spirit—namely, by demonstrations of healing and transformed lives rather than by logic and philosophy.

This approach was the same as that used by Moses when he came up against the magicians of Pharaoh and won the confrontation by demonstrating God's power:

> The LORD said to Moses and Aaron, "When Pharaoh says to you, 'Perform a miracle,' then say to Aaron, 'Take your staff and throw it down before Pharaoh,' and it will become a snake." So Moses and Aaron went to Pharaoh and did just as the LORD commanded. Aaron threw his staff down in front of Pharaoh and his officials, and it became a snake. Pharaoh then summoned wise men and sorcerers, and the Egyptian magicians also did the same things by their secret arts: Each one threw down his staff and it became a snake. But Aaron's staff swallowed up their staffs.
>
> Exodus 7:8–12

In the same way, the early Christians continued to show the pagans that Jesus could free them from the cruel domination of those evil spirits that had ruled their lives. "Our God is stronger than your god and we will demonstrate it. When we pray for you, our God will free you." Ordinary people, believing that the Gospel presented them with stark choices, also believed that a power encounter between God and Satan was needed to prove the truth. The people in those days "took miracles quite for granted. That was the general starting point. *Not* to believe in them would have made you seem more than odd."[18]

Driving all competition from the field head-on was crucial. The world, after all, held many dozens and hundreds of gods. Choice was open to everybody. It could thus be only a most exceptional force that would actually displace alternatives and compel allegiance; it could be only the most probative demonstrations that would work. We should therefore assign as much weight to this, the chief instrument of conversion, as the best, earliest reporters do.[19]

This approach reminds us of the classic Western movie with its final shoot-out on Main Street. We see the courageous hero walking slowly down the center of the dusty street while the villain marches toward him. Then comes the moment of truth when they whip out their six-shooters. The hero shoots straight and true, while the evil destroyer of the peace misses the mark and falls. Everyone in town can come out of hiding, and peace and justice reign once again: The evil has been destroyed.

Although the idea of solving disputes by killing your opponents is hardly Christian, the black-and-white image of good versus evil is easy to understand, and we take delight when the virtuous triumph.

So, gradually, person by person, Christianity spread throughout the Roman Empire.

> The manhandling of demons—humiliating them, making them howl, beg for mercy, tell their secrets, and depart in a hurry—served a purpose quite essential to the Christian definition of monotheism: it made physically (or dramatically) visible the superiority of the Christian's patron Power over all others. One and only one was God. The rest were *daimones* demonstrably, and therefore already familiar to the audience as nasty, lower powers that no one would want to worship anyway.[20]

Dr. MacMullen states unequivocally that the main ways Rome was converted to Christianity were healing and, most especially, exorcism.[21] *Contra factum non est argumentum*—"against a fact there can be no argument"—is an ancient axiom of logic.

And the facts were simple: Christ's Kingdom had come to earth, and they could prove it.

Whether or not Christians today understand that worldview, the point to make here is that's how it happened. That is how Christianity got established. If you have ever been a missionary in the Third World, you will realize that the same approach still works.

Here I am reminded of an invitation I once received from a pastor in India, asking me to come to his little village. This is the gist of what he wrote:

> Please, just come. Our people are very poor. All I want you to do is to heal the sick and cast out evil spirits in the name of Jesus. Then tell the people that the Kingdom of God is at hand.

If you received such a letter, what would your answer be? We cannot help but recognize that this pastor has caught the basic Gospel message. Aside from the problem of getting to India, our answer might well be, "Yes, I'll come."

This is simply to say that the early Church carried out Jesus' simple program of using the power of the Spirit to proclaim that the Kingdom of God is here, the kingdom of Satan is being destroyed. You can only make it work by healing wounded, hurting people and casting out evil spirits.[22]

For those hundreds of years healing was very much alive and well.

And then the powerful Emperor Constantine was converted. With the new acceptance of Christianity in the Roman Empire, everything began to change.

We will continue in the next section with our historical look at the near-death of the healing ministry through centuries of misguided emphasis. First, however, I want to give an overview of the change in attitude that took place at baptism—and how the power of the Holy Spirit began to be less welcome.

PART 3

HOW THE NEARLY PERFECT CRIME WAS COMMITTED

10

THE CHURCH UNPLUGS THE POWER

Several years ago I baptized a young woman by immersion, surrounded by about a hundred witnesses. After I had immersed her in a pool, saying the words of baptism, I noticed that she was gently trembling. The weather was hot and the water was warm, so she wasn't shivering with the cold. On the contrary, the trembling seemed to be a phenomenon we often see when a person is deeply touched by the Spirit. So I suggested to her that she might be able to pray in tongues if she wished. And so she did—trembling with joy she prayed in tongues for the first time.

And that's the way it used to happen in the early apostolic Church. Manifestations of the presence of the Holy Spirit—tongues, joyfulness, prophetic words, visions—were regarded as normal.

But gradually, for reasons we shall explore, they became the exception; visions and healings came to be associated with especially holy people. Instead of the charismatic gifts being seen as ordinary, they came to be seen as rare and as proof that a Christian was deserving of sainthood. The truly holy people, such as the desert fathers, including St. Anthony, fled from the corruption of the cities, but they also turned away from praying for the sick: They did not want to appear proud, as if they felt themselves worthy of sainthood.

When you think about it, however, this idea that the charisms are rare opposes Paul's teaching in 1 Corinthians 12:4–30, when he states that we need all these powerful gifts to build up the Body of Christ, the Church. Paul did not expect every individual to express all of the gifts, but he did expect that the community would, as a group, have all of them. They are all parts of the body, all necessary. "The eye cannot say to the hand, 'I don't need you!' And the head cannot say to the feet, 'I don't need you!'" (1 Corinthians 12:21). He also said that the least honored parts of the body are the most indispensable (by implication the least honored but necessary gift is tongues). Included among the gifts necessary to build up the Church are healing and the gift of miracles. And yet, by the fourth century, the truly committed spiritual leaders were turning from exercising the very charisms that Paul said the Church needs.

In the meantime, churches continued to baptize adults and infants, but the authorities concentrated on the symbolism of the rite and put less and less expectation on what might happen when the Holy Spirit was poured out. As Christianity became the norm, and most babies were baptized, there were also fewer and fewer adults to be baptized. And, certainly, no one expected the infants to prophesy or speak in tongues. Also, Christianity became acceptable and normative. The fervor died down and whole tribes, like the Franks, were converted and baptized as a group because it was socially acceptable—or even forced. More and more nominal Christians appeared in the churches, forcing fervent Christians, like the desert hermits, to flee their company and form new, idealistic communities.

By the eighth century baptism was no longer expected to be a Pentecost experience, especially because, by now, most Christians had been baptized as infants. In the Western Church, confirmation (for adults) was separated from baptism (ordinarily for infants), and no longer was it really clear what was supposed to happen when people were confirmed. Expectations diminished, and the results of this lack of expectancy remain with us today.

Most Christians from a sacramental tradition, for instance, do not have a clear view of what happened when they were confirmed by a bishop. Some, if pressed, might relate it to being good soldiers for

Christ. This is because in some confirmation ceremonies, the bishop is supposed to "slap" the confirmands across the cheek to symbolize that they should stand up courageously if they are ever persecuted. (This action, while memorable, is not central to the rite of confirmation.) Beyond that, most people say that they did not feel much different afterward. I remember eminent evangelist Derek Prince once saying that, so far as he was concerned, absolutely nothing took place during the Anglican service when he was confirmed as a member of the Church.

Now, I personally believe that something does happen at baptism and confirmation. I met one Roman Catholic bishop who remembers seeing tongues of fire descend on all the other young people who were being confirmed with him. And yet, when he started to share this experience, he found, to his disappointment, that no one else had seen the fire. So he learned not to talk about this marvelous event, for fear of being seen as a fanatic.

Of course, most evangelical Christians come from Protestant churches that do not hold a rite of confirmation for adults who were baptized as infants, but, rather, confer adult baptism ("believer's baptism"). They may have a hard time fitting what so many people have experienced in the "baptism with the Holy Spirit" into their theology. They, like those from a Catholic tradition, believe that they already received the Holy Spirit when they accepted Jesus Christ, so, talking about a subsequent baptism seems to deny the reality of their baptism or of having had a "born again experience."

The theoretical considerations in all of this are immense and cause all kinds of difficulties. In the practical, human order, though, the simple question seems to be, Is there something more that needs to happen so that I can experience a deeper relationship with God and so that I can be more strongly empowered to help other people?

It helped me sort out all these problems when Agnes Sanford and three other friends prayed for me to receive the baptism of the Spirit. She prayed that the Spirit would release in me all the gifts that were rooted in my baptism, confirmation and ordination. As I mentioned earlier, when they prayed I was filled with joy and laughter and, after that, my life changed in substantial ways. Just to take one example, I started praying for the sick and many were healed. My life was turned upside down, and yet the prayer for the baptism with the Spirit did not deny anything that had gone before.

And yet, I think it is fair to say that many, if not most, people in mainline churches—Protestant and Catholic—have not experienced a personal Pentecost. These are good, exemplary Christians who love the Lord—just as the apostles were before Pentecost, doing many good things under Jesus' authority—but something has not happened to allow them to move fully in the Holy Spirit's power. They are dutiful, loyal, committed, attending church every Sunday, but not filled with a sense that they could pray for the sick and have anything change.

In other words, I believe that something happens spiritually at baptism and/or confirmation but it is usually not at the level that we need. Why? I'm not sure. Perhaps it is our lack of belief, our lack of expectation, our lack of understanding of who the Holy Spirit is. Thus, we encounter the ninth Beatitude: "Blessed are those who expect nothing, for they shall not be disappointed."

Over and over, I have seen people experience the graces of Pentecost in life-transforming ways. Many of them were already earnest Christians, but there was more life in store for them. For some, long-standing moral problems were suddenly overcome through the Spirit's help; others began to see the sick healed when they prayed; pastors found themselves speaking more personally about Jesus and less about abstract topics. Almost all experienced a much closer personal relationship with Jesus.

But let me add an important word of caution: We need to be very careful not to judge the spiritual state of other people. We are so prone to judge, and this is especially true in this area: "Is your pastor Spirit-filled?" I have known many Christians who have never even heard about the baptism with the Spirit, but who demonstrate most of the signs of having been filled with the Spirit. I remember one nun, in particular, who prayed in tongues in her dreams. She was mystified about what was going on while she slept, until she attended a charismatic prayer meeting and heard a talk on the gift of tongues. After that she brought her gift into the light of day.

So far as I can see, some people who are not "charismatic" seem to be more loving, more committed, more honest in their business dealings than some charismatic or Pentecostal Christians who are eager to share their spiritual experiences at the slightest provocation.

Nevertheless, while we should be loathe to judge any individual, I think we can still say that those who pray to receive the baptism with the Holy Spirit usually find a big difference in their lives. My experience has been that most mainline Protestants and Catholics, in comparing their lives before and after their baptisms in the Spirit, will tell you that they have had life-changing experiences. It is not just an emotional time, a falling to the floor, an ecstatic gift of tongues. Any emotions are just the surface expression of a spiritual earthquake. They laugh because they feel the emotional oppression of years suddenly lift off; they rest on the floor because they are overwhelmed by the manifest presence of God.

At the time this book is being written, the greatest tourist attraction in Toronto, Canada, is the Toronto Airport Christian Fellowship, an evangelical charismatic church that thousands of people travel long distances to visit. There they receive a "refreshing," an empowerment of the Spirit. The most significant fact is that some 18 percent of these visitors are *pastors*, who come from as far away as Korea. They know they need more—not larger congregations or salaries, but more of the Spirit. The church building is not the attraction; it is not like the Cathedral of Chartres. It is a large warehouse with folding chairs set up in rows on a concrete floor.

And yet thousands come.

And these are the groups of Christians that are growing in numbers—churches that combine evangelical Christianity with the power of the Spirit—and they are growing with amazing speed.[1]

To sum it up: We do not want to deny the value and blessings of traditional Christianity over the centuries. But we have lost so much. And our churches need to be humble enough to admit it. One of the main things, really, that has been lost is the full power of the Holy Spirit in our lives. We still teach correct doctrines about the Spirit. But as Paul predicted, although we retain the right doctrines, the correct words, we have lost much of the inner power of true religion.

How did this affect the near death of the healing ministry?

In a most profound way. The entire basis of healing and liberation from evil spirits is the power of the Holy Spirit. If we don't exercise that, healing won't take place. Certainly, it will not take place as frequently. If Jesus Himself sought the baptism in the Spirit, who are we to think that we can do without it? In His humanity, in order to be the Christ ("the Anointed One"), as we have said, He started His mission at the Jordan when He was baptized in the Holy Spirit with God's power.

> God had anointed him with the Holy Spirit and with power, and because God was with him, Jesus went about doing good and curing all who had fallen into the power of the devil.
>
> Acts 10:38, JB

That is Peter's thumbnail sketch of the life of Jesus. And once we ourselves are transformed and become a new creation, the Spirit helps us to pass on this new life to others by praying for them, in turn, to be empowered. "The glory of God is a human being full alive" (St. Irenaeus).

Jesus Himself began His ministry by proclaiming the power behind His mission: "The Spirit of the Lord is on me, because he has anointed me" (Luke 4:18).

To sum it up in a few words: The power behind Jesus' mission is the power of God, the Holy Spirit.

If you disconnect any belief in the source of it all, the power of the Spirit, you naturally disconnect any belief in its effects, such as healing the sick. By the year 800—more or less—a desire for baptism with the Holy Spirit had disappeared, although individuals throughout the ages still experienced its reality.

A lively understanding of the Holy Spirit's activity was dying down; multitudes of Christians were baptized as infants but never prayed subsequently for an empowering of the Spirit. And in that same historical period an expectant belief in healing the sick was also dying out. The two are intimately connected: If the power behind healing prayer is not there, or is diminished, then fewer people will be healed. The easiest explanation—a convenient excuse—is simply, "God doesn't want to heal people anymore." Healing becomes rare and unusual.

This was one ax at the root of the tree. Connected to the loss of healing came a certain loss of compassion, the subject of our next chapter. Year after year both chipped away at the root. And when you cut the root, as we will see, the tree topples.

11

FORGOTTEN MOTIVES

Compassion and Witness to the Truth

God seems to pour out His power to heal the sick for two basic reasons: (1) it shows His love and compassion for His sick children, and (2) miraculous healing also serves as a witness to the truth.

Love and truth are both involved in miraculous healing.

Pointing to the Truth

Gradually, however, almost imperceptibly, the truth element comes to overshadow the emphasis on God's compassion and love. In the early days of Christianity, healing and deliverance showed that there was only one true God who was demonstrably more powerful than the false gods of the pagans—who were identified with demons. Miracles also identified Jesus as the long-awaited Messiah.

But when Christianity saw itself as triumphant, the need for miracles as proof died out. What remained of an emphasis on proof now concentrated on showing that certain holy people were saints and that their lives should be held up as models for the rest of us. Once the Church had been successfully established, the need for proof was mostly gone. Church leaders felt that there was no longer much need for signs and wonders.

At the beginning of the Protestant Reformation in the sixteenth century, the Roman Catholic Church stated that miracles proved it alone was the "One True Church" and publicized the healings that took place at famous shrines. As an example of this mind-set, in the early 1950s, I still remember the text on the nature of the Church that we studied in my Catholic seminary. Even then I questioned the truth of a particular footnote: It stated that God worked miracles among Catholics to show that they embodied the One True Church, and that miracles of healing would not be found among the Protestants because their churches were in error. (As for the Orthodox Church, the text stated that God might work miracles there, because although there was a split between the Roman Catholics and the Orthodox, there was no heresy involved.) At that time I had no clue that I would later learn about the reality of the healing ministry in our day through Protestant friends!

By the time I was ordained (1956), the need for miracles was still seen as a help to convince unbelievers. Shrines like Lourdes were a testimony to the reality of faith, and a medical bureau was established there with rigorous qualifications to test and judge if any healing was genuinely miraculous. Thousands of healings took place, but proven miracles are rare. On average, only one healing about every two years is attested by the doctors there as being beyond the forces of nature and incontestably supernatural and miraculous.

In 1975 I spent several hours discussing all these issues with the physician in charge of the Medical Bureau at Lourdes, Dr. Theodore Mangiapan. He told me that while he saw value in gathering this scientific testimony, still it was frustrating for him and the other doctors to spend hours upon hours examining thousands of sick pilgrims, only to come up with one valid miracle every other year that met the stringent conditions established by the commission. They saw thousands of patients who were healed; it's only that they could not prove scientifically that only God could account for it. Furthermore, he faced the additional frustration of meeting the skepticism of many present-day theologians who no longer believe in the possibility of anything miraculous. Form-criticism and the demythologizing of Scripture were gaining ground, and many theologians thought that we should drop the category of "miracle" altogether.

Even among conservative Christians, who believe in the possibility of miraculous healing, we often find the view that faith should stand alone without the aid of miracles. Those who have true belief in an unseen reality, they argue, don't need to seek miraculous proof for their faith. I remember talking with one of my friends about some of the healings I was hearing about. He claimed emphatically that he was above any need for testimonies of healing; his faith was stronger and purer than that!

And yet Paul saw healing the sick as having value in pointing the way to truth. Paul did not hesitate to compare himself with those Christian evangelists whom he did not respect:

> Though I am a nobody, there is not a thing these arch-apostles have that I do not have as well. You have seen done among you all the things that mark the true apostle, unfailingly produced: the signs, the marvels, the miracles.
>
> 2 Corinthians 12:11–12, JB

Healing was a sign that led people to believe that Jesus might be the Messiah. The crowds were saying, "When the Christ comes, will he do more miraculous signs than this man?" (John 7:31).

So, clearly, signs and wonders, the amazing part of the healings, are of major importance in the Gospel story. The healings awaken our wonder and our minds to the truth of who Jesus is.

Even so, using the event of healing as intellectual proof somehow, over the course of centuries, ended up as the only purpose for healing that had any value. And then even that became a sign of weak faith.

God's Compassion

We also lost another main motive for healing: God's compassion for His sick and wounded children. Love as a motive will always remain, as long as human beings—God's children—remain sick, wounded and hurting. Jesus often healed people because He was moved with compassion, even when it was against His best interests. How else can we explain why He healed on the Sabbath when it turned the religious leaders against Him?

If he was trying to prove that He was the Messiah, He was choosing the wrong tactic by antagonizing the very people He needed to convince: the priests, the scribes and the elders. "But the synagogue official was indignant because Jesus had healed on the sabbath" (Luke 13:14, JB). As we established earlier, we could make a good case that the main reason Jesus was condemned to death was because He continually broke the law by healing the sick on the Sabbath. He did it to show that God's love was more important than the restrictions of law and that Abba, the God He knew, was very different from the legalistic God the religious leaders worshiped.

And then we remember the times He healed the sick in private. He would sometimes say something like, "Please don't tell anyone that I healed you." He did this for one of two reasons. One, He did not want people to know that He was the Messiah—at least, just not yet (the "Messianic Secret")—because their ideal of a military, warrior Messiah clashed with His own understanding of the Messiah as being the Suffering Servant. This was to be His destiny, a loser in the eyes of the world.

Or two—another possibility—Jesus was besieged by so many multitudes of the sick that the testimony of one more witness would swell an already overwhelming crowd. He often had to escape the multitudes in order to have time to pray and to teach His disciples.

In the first chapter of Mark, we read that Jesus—long before dawn—got up, left the house and went off to a lonely place to pray. Jesus had not even told the disciples where He was going. Frustrated, Simon Peter went out looking for Him at dawn and, after finding Him, exclaimed, "Everyone is looking for you!" Jesus simply said, "Let us go somewhere else—to the nearby villages—so I can preach there also."

If you have spent much time in the healing ministry, actually praying for the sick, you have experienced just this situation of finding it difficult to have time alone with the Father or rest or eat or even reach your next ministry destination. How well I remember such times with our teams among crowds of needy people imploring us to touch them! One of the most vivid memories was when I was in Nigeria in 1974. We had ministered in one city and I was to speak in another city the next day. It broke our hearts, but we had to slip out a side door of the residence where we were staying and leave before dawn because about thirty sick people were already waiting outside the front door hoping to see us.

Thirty years ago, in one of my books, I wrote a whole chapter on the pain of having to say no[1] because you are torn between on the one hand wanting to pray for all the sick who present themselves and on the other hand your own limitations: You have to rest, you have to get away from time to time. Just to be able to write this book you are now reading, I had to beg off praying for some individuals who have been phoning the office.

As you read the gospels you realize how often Jesus tried to get away—and sometimes did. His favorite tactic seems to have been to travel into Gentile territory, such as Tyre and Sidon, where most people avoided Him and His disciples because they were Jewish. You see His very human need because "a crowd of many thousands had gathered, so that they were trampling on one another" (Luke 12:1). Other times,

> he took them with him and they withdrew by themselves to a town called Bethsaida, but the crowds learned about it and followed him. He welcomed them and spoke to them about the kingdom of God, and healed those who needed healing.
>
> Luke 9:10–11

In other words Jesus tried to go off alone, but when He actually saw the people, His compassionate heart went out to them and He once again started to teach and to heal the sick. What impelled Jesus to heal was not His desire to prove a point; it was simply because He loved people. He told His disciples, "Anyone who has seen me has seen the Father" (John 14:9). When we see Jesus' passion to heal, we are getting a glimpse of God's passion—His compassion—to cure the sick and to free those oppressed by evil spirits. Jesus told us that God is our Abba, our loving father. We know how much we desire to help our own children when they are sick and hurting. Jesus tells us that we, evil as we are, know how to give good things to our children, and so, "how much more will your Father in heaven give good gifts to those who ask him!" (Matthew 7:11).

Whatever happened to the primary reason why Jesus healed people: His love and His compassion? He still has the power to heal the sick and to set free the prisoners. He made a big point of passing it on to His disciples, and eventually to us. Today.

The sick around us now are just as numerous, hurting just as much, stretching out their hands for help. And there are millions more. If healing prayer still works, how can we justify its neglect?

But that is precisely what happened.

To summarize, we see in Jesus' example two reasons for healing the sick:

(1) to indicate through working miracles that something is true: the *truth* dimension
(2) to free God's children from sickness simply because it hurts God—and us—to see them suffer: the heart, the *love* dimension

Since the power of the Spirit is still real, and the reasons for healing are still valid, and the sick cry out in overwhelming multitudes, why did the ministry of healing and deliverance, so clearly outlined in the Gospel, nearly disappear?

This is a question that all Christians, all churches, should be asking. Let us explore the answer.

12

THE MAJOR DECLINE

Plato and the Pagans

To destroy a belief as central to Christianity as healing was, the change had to take place so gradually that Christians didn't even realize that they had lost anything.[1]

In Part 2 we saw how, for the first three centuries of Christianity, healing prayer was an ordinary practice; any and every Christian had the confidence to pray for the sick. How ironic then that just when Christianity emerged from the catacombs victorious, following the vicious persecutions, healing and deliverance prayer started sliding down the slope into insignificance.

The most important factor was, perhaps, the natural lapse from fervor. After the emperor Constantine was converted in the year 312, it became more or less fashionable to be a Christian. No longer were Christians threatened with death; no longer did it require great courage to worship God. Pagan temples, like the Pantheon in Rome, were converted into churches.

As the Church grew into its new status, many of its leaders learned to rely more on the power of possessions and political force and less on spiritual power. Along with the need to build churches and to guide and organize untold thousands of followers, there came a need to choose gifted administrators to regulate and to set everything in order. Many governmental officials of Roman provinces were now chosen to be bishops because of their business experience. The best minds were occupied in the great controversies of the day about the nature of Christ—about who was a heretic and who wasn't.

Church leaders became aware of the diminishing fervor and, to counteract it, marked out certain heroes of the faith, the saints, to encourage ordinary Christians to "climb the ladder of perfection" and imitate their lives. The first canonized saints, whose heroism was undoubted, were the martyrs who had died rather than renounce their faith.

This idea of honoring spiritual heroes was well received, but in this new era believers were no longer being martyred for their faith. Who now could be held up as Christian heroes? It seemed natural to choose those fervent men and women who imitated the martyrs by enduring the greatest sufferings; their sufferings showed that they, too, would have been ready to die as Christian witnesses. The most celebrated heroes of all were the ascetics who fled to the desert to escape the sinful cities. They fasted and took on all kinds of extraordinary penance, offering their pains in union with the sufferings of Christ—in reparation for their own sins and for the sins of the world.

One of those saints who endured extraordinary penance was St. Simon Stylites, who spent most of his life on a pillar; another was St. Anthony, who fled into the desert to fight the demons in fierce combat (his life was written up in a famous biography by St. Athanasius).

This tended to create two levels of Christians:

(1) ordinary Christians, who lived in the world, got married and tried to abide by the Ten Commandments
(2) heroic Christians who abandoned all "worldly" enjoyments, who lived celibate lives and spent long hours in prayer, fasting and penance. Some of these extraordinary spiritual athletes were singled out for recognition by the Church and were canonized as saints with a capital S

Later, the rules for officially canonizing a saint emphasized two points:

(1) the candidate had lived a *heroically* virtuous life
(2) several *miracles* were performed after the saint's death to show God's stamp of approval on the saint's life

In many ways this was a marvelous solution to the problem of the growing worldliness of Christians (St. Augustine was converted by reading the life of St. Anthony), but this particular idea of sanctity helped to destroy the common practice of praying for healing.

For instance, if you were really serious about living as a committed Christian, you might regard your suffering and sickness as an opportunity to grow in sanctity rather than as a curse—the wounding of your humanity—a curse that Jesus had come to conquer and overcome.

It turned the whole meaning of suffering and sickness upside down. Sickness came to be seen as a *blessing* permitted—if not actually sent—as a test by God in order to help you grow in holiness.

I often meet sick people who don't want anyone to pray for them, because they feel that by asking for health they are taking the easy way out and losing out on a God-given opportunity to grow in grace. (And yet, these same people go to see their doctors for treatment, and see no contradiction.)

Others will accept healing prayer, but deep down they believe that God probably wants them to remain sick as a test of their love. Even more tragic, this patient acceptance of suffering reflects an underlying harsh, severe idea of what God is like. What kind of human father or mother would inflict sickness and pain on his or her child in order to test the child's goodness? In human terms, we instantly judge that parent to be a child-abuser.

It is certainly true to say that someone who endures great suffering for the sake of a deeply held truth is a witness, a martyr, for that truth. And Jesus promised His followers that they would suffer—perhaps even unto death—but the danger is that we see the suffering, the sickness, as a blessing in itself. One author claimed that a half-truth is like a half-brick; when you throw it, it goes farther. The main sign of holiness is still love: "By this all men will know that you are my disciples, if you love one another" (John 13:35). And although the willingness to suffer martyrdom is a great sign of heroism, still it is not a test that all of us are asked to undergo. "If I give away all that I possess, piece by piece, and if I even let them take my body to burn it, but am without love, it will do me no good whatever" (1 Corinthians 13:3, JB).

The early Church taught that love had to accompany martyrdom, but I think, in our humanity, we gravitate to things we can measure. While we can never measure love directly, we can measure to a certain extent acts of heroic suffering—such as fasting throughout your life or living in a desert hermitage. The harsher the life, the more saintly it can seem. A person who remains cheerful and patient in a wheelchair can seem more holy than a totally healthy person. If you have read Catholic lives of saints, you see an enormous admiration for persons who voluntarily took on unusual penances. For instance, one saint as an infant was said to have abstained from nursing at his mother's breasts on Wednesdays and Fridays.

For some idealistic Christians, the next step after admiring heroic martyrdom and seeing suffering as a blessing was to seek after suffering. Fervent Christians began to believe that if God loved you, He would send great sufferings to test you and mark you as a saint. That killed off any desire to pray for healing. If you think that your sickness is sent by God, you will try to patiently endure it rather than to ask God to take it away. If you are a tepid Christian, you might want to get rid of your sickness, but if you are a "real" Christian, you will willingly embrace your sickness as a path to holiness.

Reinforcing this belief is a further realization that you may want to do penance for your sins. And going beyond that, if you are truly generous, you should also desire to do penance and suffer for the many other sinners in the world.

The scriptural basis for this was Paul's statement: "It makes me happy to suffer for you, as I am suffering now, and in my own body to do what I can to make up all that has still to be undergone by Christ for the sake of his body, the Church" (Colossians 1:24, JB). We can easily see that a popular view of a saint was someone who fled the pleasures of the world (including marriage) to engage in a life of great penance.

These ideals underlie some forms of Catholic spirituality and are not so common among Protestants in our day, but they are of key importance, because they were common in the post-Constantinean Church and were a factor in the decline of the healing ministry.

And this acceptance of suffering largely remained in the Roman Catholic Church. For a fairly recent example, take St. Thérèse of Lisieux (1873–1897), a French Carmelite nun, who wrote a moving autobiography, powerfully describing her love for God.[2] One morning, waking up, she discovered that she was spitting up blood.[3] Although she was only 24 years old, she was overwhelmed with joy that she might soon go to heaven and, after reporting the blood flow to her prioress, as she was required to do, she no longer complained about it.

As a result, her Carmelite sisters did not realize how serious her tuberculosis was, and they did not give her the rest and care that might have helped her to prolong her life. She was content to suffer and made her TB an offering to help missionaries. And so, she died early, as she had hoped. In this desire to suffer for Jesus' sake we clearly see her great love, and her autobiography is a spiritual classic.

The Influence of Plato

The tendency of allowing the body to suffer for the sake of the soul was increased when Christianity became popular and when sophisticated intellectuals, indoctrinated by the teachings of the great Plato, became Christian. The entire Greek and Roman cultures were influenced by Plato's thought and this, in turn, affected Christian thought. Plato saw the body as a prison from which the soul needed to escape. This devaluing of the body was absorbed into Christianity.

Christians became concerned about "saving souls"—a term you never find in the gospels. The "Kingdom of God" meant the next world—heaven. The more you virtuously suffer in this world, the more your soul will benefit in the coming life: A cross in this life—a crown in the next. The body was to be "mortified"—which literally means to be "put to death"—for the soul's sake.

Granted, our unruly passions need to be *tamed* and brought under the discipline of the Spirit, but being brought under God's rule is different from being *killed*, being mortified.

Other Pagan Influences

A host of other pagan influences flooded the civilization into which Christianity was growing. For example, the stoics taught that reason and will were all-important and the emotions were a sign of weakness to be ignored.

You may never have heard of the Manichees, and yet you are probably influenced by them more than you know. This is because St. Augustine (342–430), probably the most influential theologian during the first thousand years of Christianity, was a Manichee before his conversion to Christ. The Manichees taught that matter was basically evil, especially in regard to our sexuality. Augustine wrote that nothing dragged a man down from the heights of spirituality more than the embraces of a woman, and he brought some of this attitude with him when he became a Christian. The body, again, was seen as somehow evil, drawing people away from the spirit.

Origen (ca. 250) carried this tendency to its extreme, for he castrated himself, basing his drastic action on Jesus' remarks that some followers make themselves eunuchs for the Kingdom of God. Instead of seeing the material universe—and the human body—as God's beloved creation, it was seen as something close to being an enemy.

Sexual intercourse, even between married partners, came to be viewed as sinful—seriously sinful for the unmarried; but, even for the married, theologians considered sex as venially sinful. Sexual pleasure was allowed only because of the need to procreate children. The pleasure, being strong as well as delectable, was what was seen as dangerous, since it clouded the mind and the spirit (a stoic attitude).

Belief in healing of our spirits still remained—such as when God forgives our sins—but this takes place invisibly in our souls rather than in our bodies. The spiritual aspect of healing remained as strong as ever. But the body was something else.

Christians today are afraid of New Age influences. What many don't realize is that we are often deeply influenced by what might be called Old Age paganism. Pope St. Gregory the Great (pope from 590–604 and one of the eight great "doctors of the Church") taught that married couples could copulate only with the express purpose of having children, otherwise they were sinning. He went still further by teaching that any pleasure that was experienced in marital intercourse was still a sin. Not only was the *pursuit* of pleasure in intercourse unlawful, but if any pleasure was "mixed" with the act of intercourse, the married had "transgressed the law of marriage."[4]

The couple's sin would be a small one; nevertheless, they would have "befouled" their intercourse through experiencing pleasure. For this reason they were to abstain from going to church or receiving Communion the next day. (The beginnings of mandatory celibacy for priests go back to those days, but that is another story.)

The Conflict Within

For years I struggled with these concepts in my own life, since as a young man, a Roman Catholic, I wanted to be holy, to be a saint. The ideal that I somehow absorbed was pretty grim; I felt guilty when I spent any time for myself on vacation or in simple pleasures. I read St. Augustine's *Confessions*, where he blames himself for wasting time watching a rabbit running across the grass when he could have been praying.

Then when I learned about praying for healing, I had to sort out the meaning of suffering. In my earlier books, *Healing*[5] and *The Power to Heal*,[6] I try to deal with this entire question—which is so important—about what our attitude toward sickness should be.

Jesus' passion was to heal: He treated sickness as a curse. Jesus suffered to an extraordinary degree, and He promised His followers that they would suffer, too. But the suffering we can expect is what will be inflicted upon us by a hostile and fallen world, not the kind of suffering that happens because we fall apart from within ourselves through spiritual, emotional and bodily sickness. Nowhere do we have a record of Jesus telling sick people who came to Him for healing that He was not going to heal them because their sickness was a blessing sent by His Father as a test of patience.

The entire 28th chapter of Deuteronomy is composed of the blessings that will come to those who keep the Law and curses for those who refuse to listen. And a large part of those curses (Deuteronomy 28:21–29) involves sickness. Much of it is physical: "The LORD will afflict you with the boils of Egypt and with tumors, festering sores and the itch, from which you cannot be cured" (Deuteronomy 28:27).

Some of it is emotional: "The LORD will afflict you with madness, blindness and confusion of mind. At midday you will grope about like a blind man in the dark. You will be unsuccessful in everything you do" (Deuteronomy 28:28–29). These curses were not sent to faithful followers of Yahweh as signs of favor; the people who chose evil would reap the consequences of their sin.

Jesus did not promise a comfortable life! But He never told us to embrace sickness, physical or emotional. He certainly did not encourage us to put up with demonic infestation. Instead, He promised us freedom from the kind of infirmity that prevents us from living a loving life of service. He wants us to live the kind of courageous life that will inevitably bring on the attacks and persecutions that follow an attempt to imitate Him in His speaking out against injustice, legalism and hypocrisy. This is why Paul could boast about being beaten with rods, being stoned, being shipwrecked, and going without food and sleep (see 2 Corinthians 11:23–29).

Nevertheless, because of the emphasis on penance and heroic abnegation as the heart of a truly serious Christian life, centuries passed with the belief that only weak faith would ask God to take away sickness.

If the body and the spirit are locked in combat, and the body's needs are to be put to death, it is almost impossible to see prayer for healing the body as part of our attempt to live a Christian life—especially a heroic Christian life.

13

CAUGHT IN TRANSITION

St. Augustine

From A.D. 350 on, healings became relatively rare. We have already set down some likely reasons for the decline. One major reason was that many Christians were now Christians in name only. Another was that healing came to be seen in terms of importance to the intellect, rather than to the heart (compassion). Jesus healed people because He loved people, because He was moved by compassion, because He saw the sick as beloved children of His Father. But now the emphasis shifted to healings as proof. First, they were a proof that Christianity was the true religion; then later, they became signs of the holiness of the one who prayed for the healing. Healings now were a proof of sanctity, a status that the humble did not presume to achieve.

From the fifth century on, we read many testimonies of healing. But no longer did the believer talk with the sick person, make up his own prayer tailored to the sick person's need and, together with the laying on of hands, trust that God's power might be transmitted by the human touch. The human need for healing the sick still remained strong as ever. The sick and suffering, in their thronging multitudes, cried out for help, but they were discouraged from going to ministers of healing living on this earth. Instead, they were sent off to shrines filled with the statues of the saints and their relics.

The saints, of course, were considered to be living in heaven. (The Communion of Saints was an article of belief that would be written into the Church's creed.) There are numerous records about how the saints often appeared in visions, but they belonged to another world, and attempts to contact them directly were forbidden as spiritualism.

A personal touch was added when saints were chosen as patrons of particular diseases and infirmities, such as St. Jude, "patron of hopeless cases," and St. Dymphna, "patroness of the mentally ill." We read of numerous testimonies of healings attributed to these specialized saints and their shrines.

But mostly we lost the human touch. A statue of a saint cannot substitute for a living human being who can talk to you. How can you perform a deliverance from evil spirits without a human exorcist present? After the fourth century, occasional exorcisms occurred, because religious authorities still realized that a direct confrontation is necessary to free a possessed person from the domination of an evil spirit. Nevertheless, the deliverance ministry was restricted: Eventually only priests were allowed to perform exorcisms. A few centuries later, things became even more narrowly restricted: A priest had to receive permission from his bishop to exorcise someone, and the individual had to be proven to be possessed—a rare occasion!

The idea of making pilgrimages to shrines was not unfamiliar; it fit into the pattern of the pre-Christian pagan culture, when the sick would visit the shrine of Aesculepius or Diana and spend the night, seeking a prophetic dream or inspiration and hoping to wake in the morning cured. In these new shrines, appeals to the old gods were replaced by appeals to the Christian God, mediated by the intercession of the saints.

Soon the sick were making pilgrimages to these holy shrines dedicated to their favorite local saints—or, even better, to those internationally known, such as the Shrine of St. Nicholas of Bari (who eventually became "Santa Claus"). If you have read Chaucer's *Canterbury Tales,* you know that these pilgrimages were a great source of fun and recreation in the often-grim Middle Ages. This does not mean that some of the people who went on pilgrimages to shrines did not get well, but they were deprived of all the advantages of individual, personal prayer.

From the point of view of the priests, who might be approached by the sick begging for healing prayer, this referral system had three distinct human advantages:

(1) Priests—and laypeople, as well—no longer had to struggle with the issue of pride.
(2) They didn't have to spend lengthy sessions praying with the sick.
(3) They didn't have to answer the ever-present embarrassing question as to why some sick persons were not healed when they prayed. They were no longer personally responsible for any results.

Humanly, we can understand why these early Christians stopped praying for healing, particularly regarding the third reason above. We are all uncomfortable with mystery. We cannot explain why some people are healed and others are not. We look for clear answers and there aren't any. We are embarrassed when we pray for healing and then nothing seems to happen. We can always say, "It's not God's will for you to be healed." But how can anyone be sure of that? The answer really is, "I don't know."

How much easier to get out of the quandary by sending the person over to a shrine to pray in the presence of the saint's statue or their relics!

This is the world into which Augustine was born.

Teaching of the Times

St. Augustine, generally regarded as the greatest theologian of the first thousand years of Church history, underwent some momentous changes in his understanding of miraculous healing. His life remarkably mirrors that time of confusion when the attitude changed from "everyone gets to play" to hardly anyone, anymore, dares to pray for healing.

He came on the scene roughly one hundred years after Constantine's conversion and the subsequent toleration of Christianity by the Roman Empire. His early life (detailed in his famous *Confessions*) was spoiled by self-indulgence, and he adhered to the cult of the Manichees.

His conversion to Christianity, which he credits to the prayers of his mother, Monica, came about through reading the life of St. Anthony of the Desert and picking up Paul's letter to the Romans. Regarding the latter, he heard a little boy chanting, "Tolle, lege": "Pick up and read." He opened to the first chapter and read eagerly that famous passage where Paul describes the depravity and wickedness of the human race without God.

Under the tutelage of the great bishop of Milan, St. Ambrose (who was once a Roman administrator of a province), Augustine embraced Christianity. Once he made his decision, he went all out in his new life, abandoning his mistress and forming a little community of dedicated friends with his son, Adeodatus (meaning "given by God").

For us, the significant thing is that Augustine learned Christian practice as it was then taught (around 380), which means that he was not taught to pray for healing. Theologians now believed that the days of healing miracles had mostly ceased: an early stage of Cessationism. In his early writings he stated that Christians were not to look for a continuation of healing miracles. Miracles might possibly take place, but don't expect them.

And yet the sick people themselves were not to be denied; they still continued to seek divine healing, as they always have throughout human history.

Miracles Happen

To take care of these clamoring sick people, the solution in the fifth century, as we have noted, was to send them to a shrine. From the point of view of a priest, this practice has all the advantages that we have mentioned. Thus, Augustine did what he was taught to do: When the sick came to him, he sent them off to pray at the nearby shrine of St. Stephen.

Before long, though, he discovered that a large number of miracles were taking place at the shrine. One example that amazed Augustine happened when a brother and sister, who both suffered from convulsive seizures, came to Augustine's cathedral (in Hippo, North Africa) on Easter, 424. Before the celebration of the service, the young man got hold of a relic of St. Stephen. While Augustine was still getting vested in his robes, the young man fell down as if dead. When he rose up, he found that he was healed. He had dinner with Augustine and they talked about what happened.

Three days later Augustine read the brother's testimony in church, while both the brother and his sister were standing up in front of the congregation. He now seemed quite normal, but his sister was trembling convulsively. Then, when Augustine started preaching, she slipped off to the shrine to pray. Exactly the same thing that had happened to her brother happened to her: She was healed and came back to interrupt Augustine's sermon with loud cries.

Augustine testified that "praise to God was shouted so loud that my ears could hardly stand the din. But, of course, the main point was that, in the hearts of all this clamoring crowd, there burned that faith in Christ for which the martyr Stephen shed his blood."[1] Through experiences like these, Augustine radically changed his mind and came to realize that God was still healing people—and commonly—in his day. In 426 he wrote:

> I realized how many miracles were occurring in our own day and which were so like the miracles of old and also how wrong it would be to allow the memory of these marvels of divine power to perish from among our people. It is only two years ago that the keeping of records was begun here in Hippo, and already, at this writing, we have nearly seventy attested miracles.[2]

As you can see, Augustine changed from "miracles have mostly ceased" to a position where he admitted that he was wrong and that miracles were still a common occurrence. And yet he himself still did not pray for the sick. He continued to turn the healing ministry over to the saints by sending the sick off to their shrines, thereby avoiding the risks of personally praying for healing.

But then, shortly before he died, Augustine was persuaded to put himself on the line and actually pray for a sick person. It all began when he prayed for several demoniacs who were freed (you could hardly turn an exorcism over to a deceased saint). Then he was led to take a greater risk when a friend pleaded with him to heal a sick relative, by laying hands on him. By then Augustine was suffering from his own last illness, so he replied that if he felt that he had any such ability, he would certainly have prayed for himself. But that did not convince his friend, who replied that he had received a vision in his sleep in which he heard the words, "Go to Bishop Augustine that he may lay his hand upon your sick relative, and he will be healed."[3] This prophetic approach finally convinced Augustine that he should pray in person. When at last he laid his hands on the man, he was healed!

Just three years before he died, Augustine realized that he had changed his mind on a number of matters since he had first become a Christian and, wanting to clear the record, he wrote an entire book of *Retractions*, in which he took back many of his earlier statements. One of these mistaken statements was that God did not allow miracles to continue in his time. Augustine's own experiences of healing had changed his mind as had the fact that so many healings were taking place in his city that he could no longer even count them all.[4]

These changes in Augustine's thinking reflect the confusion in his time: No longer did most ministers encourage their people to pray for healing, but Augustine's experience changed him back to the earlier view of Church history. He also stated that "not everyone today who has hands laid on them in baptism thus receives the Holy Spirit so as to speak in tongues . . . and if such things were once done, it is clear that they afterwards ceased."[5]

This makes us suspect that the dimming of the healing ministry was connected with a diminished understanding of the baptism with the Holy Spirit and the gifts of the Spirit—such as prophecy and heal-ing. Without the power of the Spirit, it is only to be expected that the charisms of the Spirit would also fade out of history.

14

HEALING GETS LOST IN CHAOS

The Barbarian at the Gate

With all of the reasons we have noted for the near-total disappearance of healing prayer, all based on faulty human thinking, one more reason is notable because it was just a fact of life in the fourth century. This was simply because the whole Roman and Middle Eastern world was immersed in violent turmoil.

At the very time Constantine was converted (312) and Christianity finally emerged from persecution, the Roman world was already falling apart. A decision had to be made as to whether or not Rome was safe enough to remain as the capitol, or if the capitol should be moved to Constantinople. The political situation was dangerous, disastrous. Pagans attributed the upheaval to the fact that they had deserted their ancient gods. Even as Augustine was dying (he died in 430) in North Africa (present-day Algeria), the barbarians were threatening the gates of Rome.

There were political reasons for Constantine's conversion, one of which was his desire to unify Rome with a single religion. To facilitate this, he more or less ordered the bishops to get their act together and agree upon a single doctrine in relation to Christ. He ordered three hundred bishops to come to a Council at his palace in Nicaea and reach an agreement, especially as to whether or not to condemn the teachings of Arius, who held that Jesus was not of the same substance as the Father, but was a created being.

The emperor Constantine was a dominant force at this Council; there was no doubt about who was in charge. He gave the opening address, commanded both sides to stop arguing over what to him seemed minor points, presided on a throne set high over the deliberations and threatened to depose any bishop who refused to accept the Council's final decrees.

> Constantine could be said to have found Christianity a religion which considered itself not of this world and to have left it a religion with an enormous worldly investment. He, more than anyone else, was responsible for making the church a temporal as well as a spiritual power, for giving it a vision of itself as responsible for bringing about the kingdom of God on earth through political, economic and military means. That vision was to prove perhaps the greatest obstacle down through the centuries to the accomplishment of the church's spiritual mission.[1]

To people in those days it almost seemed as if the universal chaos demonstrated that the world was coming to an end, in the Church as well as in the Empire. After Constantine's death, for a time the heresy of Arianism triumphed, but then another emperor, Theodosius, ordered all Christians (379) to profess the orthodox Nicene Creed reached by Constantine's Council. Shortly afterward, he convened the Council of Constantinople (381), which deposed all Arian bishops.

Force and violence were used to enforce these decisions, and in this atmosphere of controversy, survival became the focus for ordinary Christians. One barbarian tribe after another poured into Italy, and in 402 the capitol was removed to Ravenna, a small Italian town. In 476, a Germanic chief ended the Roman Empire in the West by deposing the emperor and the "Dark Ages" began.

Christendom was torn apart from within by bitter doctrinal controversies and the political unity of Rome was ending. Constantinople's leadership was also ripped into shreds. The leaders of the Church were necessarily concentrating almost all their attention upon trying to unify it, and bishops were chosen because of their administrative skills and leadership. Orthodox bishops were forced into exile by Arian bishops—and vice versa. The most famous bishop of the time, Athanasius, was forced to flee Egypt, ending up in what is now France.

Christian leaders could focus on little else other than the turmoil around them. Take Pope Leo the Great. When Attila's Huns threatened Rome (in 452), Leo rode north on a mule to talk them out of sacking Rome. Amazingly, he succeeded. Then, four years later, he persuaded Gaiseric, king of the Vandals, not to burn Rome or kill its inhabitants. They were working desperately to create some kind of order and thought of little else.

In the political sphere, feudalism arose in which every part of society found its definitive, assigned level—and these levels were believed to be ordained by God. (We still say clergy receive the gift of "orders" and are "ordained.")

At the top was the nobility, with the emperors and kings at the very pinnacle. Next down the ladder came the warriors, the knights, the military caste (such as "the Knights of Malta"). Then, at the bottom were the slaves, the serfs, the farmers, the peasant class. Most of the serfs—who were virtually slaves—worked from dawn until dark and were illiterate. With little or no leisure time, their knowledge of Jesus' teachings was confined to what they heard from their pastors on Sunday or what they saw in the religious art of their day.

Learning nearly disappeared, except as it was preserved in the royal courts of the day and in the monasteries, which were first founded in the 400s by St. Benedict and his followers, the early Benedictines.

To complete the feudal order with its three classes (nobles, warriors and peasants), the Church formed a special fourth class for religious ministry.

This special class of clerics was also divided roughly into two groups: the nobility who entered the ranks of the Church and were usually destined to be bishops. Then came the ordinary candidates for priesthood, who were slated to be parish priests. A remnant of this stratification between nobility and commoners can still be seen in the British parliament, where the bishops sit with the other nobility in the House of Lords. Just one hundred years ago my great-uncle, Francis Augustus MacNutt, was invited by Pope Leo XIII to become a seminarian in the Academy for Noble Ecclesiastics in Rome, another remnant of a bygone era. (Although the invitation was in itself an honor, he dropped out before ordination.) The graduates of the academy, from "noble" families, were slated for bishoprics and diplomatic posts in the Vatican.

Feudal society needed to set aside this special group, devoted to the work of the Church: these were the professionals, as it were, in the area of religion—they were the ones who, ideally at least, learned to read and write, who had time to devote to prayer and to minister to the vast majority of people. They preached and centered their lives on the sacraments, while the laypeople were there to receive their ministrations. Laypeople gradually became more passive. This division is still with us, although it is now changing (along with some resistance from the clergy and some from the laity). Even in the 1950s when I was in seminary, the text we studied on the meaning of the Church (*De Ecclesia* by Paris) divided it into two classes: the teaching Church (*Ecclesia docens*) and the learning Church (*Ecclesia discens*).

The teaching Church was made up of the pope, the bishops and—by extension—the priests. The group who listened, learned and obeyed were the laypeople. In the Middle Ages these distinctions made sense, because the peasants could not read or write. The word *clerk* comes from the same root as *cleric*, because only the clergy (and some of the nobility) were literate, and the repositories of learning were the monasteries. In fact, because an education was so hard to come by, many of the priests were ignorant and illiterate, one of the factors that led to the Reformation.

This setting up of a competent professional group of ministers whose lives were meant to center upon studying and teaching the Gospel began back in the early centuries. This distinction between those who minister (the "minister") and those who are ministered to has continued to influence not only Catholics but Protestants as well. Although the focus of Catholic worship is the altar, and Protestant worship came to center upon the pulpit, both groups still tend to leave the ministry to the clergy; until recently, the laypeople were left out of ministry. "Pray, pay and obey" was the way they joked about the situation.

In those ancient days (until the sixteenth century), there were no seminaries. One became a priest simply by becoming an apprentice to the parish priest who taught whatever Scripture and theology he knew, as well as how to celebrate the rituals of the liturgy. A common lament of Church authorities was the pitiful ignorance of the clergy. Preaching was in such a sad condition that southern France was being rapidly converted to a heresy called Albigensianism, which deemed much of the material world as evil.

St. Dominic founded the Dominican order, the Order of Preachers, in the thirteenth century, because priests (and even bishops) throughout Europe lacked enough knowledge of Scripture to preach effectively. Dominic wanted to found a corps of priests who studied Scripture and theology at the major universities, such as Oxford, Bologna and Paris, and could preach in-depth the truths of Christianity. Books were rare. Dominic, for example, possessed just two books of the Bible: the gospel of Matthew and Paul's letter to the Romans. And these were heavy treasures, handwritten on calfskin.

During a time of widespread wars, accompanied by a general lack of learning, it is no wonder that many of the central truths of Christianity were obscured. For most people it was a triumph simply to survive and not starve. They were happy to have a family in which ten of fifteen children survived to become adults. You were fortunate to live to the ripe old age of fifty.

The ancient practice of healing prayer simply faded away along with the general disappearance of knowledge and the prevalence of violence. The search for holiness was largely confined to the monasteries, but history records a generally disastrous leadership gap in the papacy itself. Even five hundred years before the Protestant Reformation, the

> papacy, having become the private possession of a few noble families, had entered the period of its most profound degradation. This period can be considered to have begun in 904 when Cardinal Sergius . . . seized the papal throne and had his predecessor strangled. He then took as his mistress an exceedingly ambitious teenage girl named Marozia, daughter of the Roman nobleman, Theophylactus. According to the generally reliable *Liber Pontificalis*, Sergius fathered the child whom she later made pope.[2]

Marozia then married Alberic, produced another son, and settled down to the business of running the papacy. When Pope John X entered into an alliance with Hugh of Provence, the King of the Lombards, Marozia had him deposed and murdered. (John was not a particularly unworthy pontiff by the standards of the day, although one of his more disreputable actions was to approve the consecration of a five-year-old boy as archbishop of Rheims.)

Marozia handpicked the next two popes. Then, in 931, she had her older son, who was about twenty years of age, elected as Pope John XI. Alberic meanwhile had been succeeded by his and Marozia's son, while Marozia herself had married Hugh of Provence, her third husband. (By now are you getting confused?)

She had achieved a position unique in history. One of her sons was pope; her husband, Hugh, was destined to become emperor (this was not difficult to arrange, since it was the pope who bestowed the imperial crown); and her other son, Alberic II, was in line to become emperor after Hugh. Marozia was well on the way to controlling both the papal and the imperial thrones, which would have made her one of the most powerful women who ever lived. Some historians, in fact, believe that it may have been Marozia's total domination of the papal court that gave rise to the medieval legend of Pope Joan.[3]

There were, amazingly, fervent Christians still to be found and the famous Cluniac reform of the monasteries took place at this same time. But if the main leaders are engaged in murdering each other and are more famed for avarice and lust than for holiness, we hardly need to wonder why the Kingdom of God is not proclaimed, accompanied by healings and exorcisms. The very leaders themselves seem to have been prime candidates for exorcism!

15

HEALING PRAYER IS ELEVATED OUT OF REACH

Somehow, in this utter turmoil and chaos, a certain group had to be chosen to be competent enough to carry out the teaching and praying functions of the Church. The everlasting fear of the Church has always been that, once you open the door to universal ministry, all kinds of weird apostles, teaching strange doctrines, will rise up. "You senseless Galatians," Paul had shouted out, "who has bewitched you?"

These eccentric teachers were often successful, and the discouraging fact was that there were always people, like the Galatians, eager to follow them. The major disturbances in the Church had to do with doctrine—Arianism, Docetism, Donatism, Nestorianism—leading to major divisions, and then even leading to bloodshed. And these costly disputes were led by educated theologians, including bishops.

When the Roman Empire fell to the barbarian hordes and Roman law and order gave way to chaos, with the enemies at the gate, the political order had to react and try to establish some kind of order again.

In the early Church, bishops would bless oil to be used for anointing the sick, and the laypeople would take it home and use it to anoint each other and pray for their families. Gradually, however, the anointing came to be seen as a special prerogative of the priest, whose anointing came to be considered as a sacrament—the Anointing of the Sick, which laypeople could not minister. Even in our time, some bishops forbid non-priests to use oil for anointing when they pray for the sick.

In this way, laypeople received the clear message that they were not the best ones to pray for healing. The priests were considered as having a higher calling. Although they might not be saints, by virtue of their priesthood their prayers, especially in the sacraments, were regarded as having a special effect.[1] With the power and authority of the entire Church behind them, these prayers were seen as having far more value than the prayers of any ordinary layman.

Prayer for the sick, therefore, became narrowed down to (1) the prayers of a priest, which were (2) composed and written down in liturgical books.

Regulations Are Imposed

Unfortunately, the chaos of the times in both Church and state made it necessary to establish regulations, not only as to the persons who were allowed to pray but also to the words they could say, and even gestures they were to make when praying. If you can use only the written-down prayers in the book, spontaneity is lost and the prayers have to be of a very general nature suited to all occasions. Necessarily, they become abstract rather than personal.

Until recently, this fear of making up one's own prayer has continued on. I have met many devout Christians who are embarrassed to say a spontaneous prayer. I well remember a healing conference I led some years ago in Montana for the Lakota and Assinaboin tribes of Native Americans. At one point I asked a white Catholic priest to say a prayer for reconciliation, which he did. Then I asked Joe Red Thunder, a Lakota chief, to say a prayer on behalf of the Native Americans. He had never experienced anything like this, so for a long time he was silent. At last, he hesitantly said the Lord's Prayer. (Later he was emboldened to become a lay evangelist who traveled throughout Montana and western Canada.)

In these days, more and more laypeople are becoming comfortable in making up prayers on different occasions, but just a short time ago most people felt that only ministers or priests were competent to lead prayers. Making up a spontaneous prayer for healing was even more out of the question for most Christians—and this attitude goes back more than a thousand years to the strong distinction that was set up between the clergy and laypeople.

A further block to ordinary people feeling empowered to pray came about because, for hundreds of years, the only authorized translation of Scripture was in Latin, the so-called Vulgate. When St. Jerome (ca. 342–420) made the Vulgate translation, Latin was the language of the Roman Empire. The Vulgate, however, remained the only official translation in the Catholic Church for fifteen hundred years, long after most ordinary people no longer spoke in Latin.

A further blow to prayer for physical healing took place because of a particular wording Jerome used in his translation of the famous healing text in James (see James 5:14–16). When James tells the sick person to call the elders of the church who will pray for him to be healed, Jerome translated the Greek into Latin by saying that their prayer will *save* him (not *heal* him). Since this was the only text available to most Christians until the Protestant Reformation, this change in emphasis reinforced the belief that God's power was centered on spiritual effects—on the soul—and not the body with its physical ailments.

Add to this the fact that, for the most part, only clerics and monks could read Latin. The people's link with Scripture was missing unless their preachers based their sermons on scriptural texts. The only ones who had access to the gospels were the priests and monks and even some of them were unable to read and write. When St. Dominic (ca. 1225) first read the section in Matthew about Jesus choosing the Twelve to go out and preach, he was deeply moved. He founded the Order of Preachers based upon the instructions in Matthew 10.

Unfortunately, much of Church life in the Dark Ages had to concern itself with reforming the leaders themselves, the clergy and monks. Encouraging them to pray for the sick was not a priority. The clergy needed to become intellectual leaders, at least to the extent that they knew enough to preach to the unlettered masses.

And they needed to be moral leaders, too, examples in leading the Christian life. And yet, all the way back in the fourth century, St. John Chrysostom was preaching about how the streets of hell were paved with the bald heads of priests. The next thousand years were fierce days when morality was enforced by severe discipline. For example, St. Boniface (in the eighth century) convened the first Frankish reform synod (with the backing of the Emperor Charlemagne) which decreed that

> any of the servants of God . . . falling into carnal sin shall do penance in prison on bread and water. If it be an ordained priest he shall be imprisoned for two years, first flogged to bleeding and afterward further disciplined at the bishop's discretion.[2]

The Sacrament of the Sick

In a way, making the anointing of the sick into a sacrament elevated healing to a highly honored and official ministry. But at the same time, it made healing less accessible than ever. It was put so high on a pedestal, very few could reach it.

I mentioned that people at one time took home oil that had been blessed and used it to anoint anyone who was sick. This became "holy oil" which only the priest could use to anoint. No longer could families take it home.

Healing prayer became an established, formal rite of the Church. And only the bishop or priest was permitted to pronounce the prayer over the sick. Most laypeople would not have had the audacity to pray for a friend, or even a family member, to be healed.

And then came an even further limitation, which, again, began as a worthy desire to elevate anointing the sick to the high level of a sacrament. Prayer for healing became the Anointing of the Sick, one of the seven principal liturgical rites of the Church. (Only in the twelfth century did the final list of seven come to be accepted.)

Here is how it happened. Originally, the anointing was mostly for bodily healing. But part of the teaching about a sacrament, as defined by scholastic theologians, was that it *always* had its effect, it *always* worked. Again, this seemed to honor and elevate healing prayer. If a priest pronounced the words of forgiveness, for instance, then the penitent's sins were truly forgiven (unless, of course, the penitent was not truly repentant). If the priest said the words of consecration at the Mass, then the bread and wine really did become the Body and Blood of Christ.

But we all know that if we say the words, "Be healed," over a sick person, he or she doesn't always jump up healed! Many other factors are involved. The entire situation is a mystery and healing is in no way automatic. (The original Greek word for *sacrament*, by the way, means "mystery.")

This meant that the primary purpose of this sacrament has to become something spiritual—that would always take place—and not physical, bodily healing. Thus, ironically, the main purpose of the sacrament of anointing the sick could no longer be physical healing, because bodily healing does not always take place when you pray. The effect has to be a spiritual healing, something you cannot see.

The Last Anointing

Already healing prayer has been narrowed down to priests and then only within a sacramental setting, but then—in the ninth century—the sacrament became even more drastically reduced. This happened when the Anointing of the Sick became the Last Anointing.

This Last Anointing was only to be ministered to those certain of *dying*. Its purpose was no longer for healing, but for spiritually preparing a dying person for entrance into heaven. A qualification now for receiving the sacrament was that you had to be in danger of death. The hands, the ears, the eyes—all the senses—were to be anointed to cleanse them from the remnants of sin. Not that this isn't an important, worthy purpose, but ordinary prayer for bodily healing was now removed from official Church life.

How did such a drastic change come about? Again, the change took several hundred years, and it came about precisely because prayer for healing had become elevated to the level of a sacrament.

One of the conditions for receiving a sacrament in the Roman Catholic tradition is that the person needs first of all to be forgiven of any serious sin to be worthy of receiving it. This meant that if you wanted to receive the sacramental Anointing of the Sick, you first of all needed to receive another one of the seven sacraments, the Sacrament of Confession (now called the Sacrament of Reconciliation). The penance that was given out in those early centuries (between 600 and 1200, when these developments took place) became codified in the "Penitentiaries" (which were books listing the penance to be given out for each particular sin). These were so severe that people put off going to confession until the end of their lives, when they were excused from doing penance because they were too feeble and sickly to perform them.

Just to give you an idea of what a penance was like, look at these taken from the *Roman Penitential* (written by Bishop Halitgar, ca. 830):

- A priest who commits natural fornication shall do penance for three years, and shall ask pardon every hour and fast every week, except during the days between Easter and Pentecost.
- Everyone who brings about abortion shall do penance for three years, one year on bread and water.
- If anyone commits perjury through cupidity, he shall sell all his goods and give to the poor and be shaven and enter a monastery; and there he shall serve faithfully until death.
- Those who kiss simply shall do penance with seven special fasts; for lascivious kissing without pollution, eight special fasts, but with pollution or embrace they shall be corrected with fifteen special fasts.[3]

No wonder people put off calling the priest to go to confession until they were on the brink of death! Because confession had to come first, they also put off asking for the sacrament of Anointing the Sick, which, in any case, was no longer intended primarily to bring about physical healing. Since now the sick person had to be in danger of death in order to receive the Anointing of the Sick, it was called the Last Anointing or Extreme Unction (*extreme* meaning the last), hence the Last Rites. Physical healing was still seen as possible but was no longer expected, especially since the patient was dying; bodily healing was only regarded as a secondary effect.

Think of the irony of all this! If you are sick but not in danger of death, you cannot receive prayers for your healing. And you might not want to if you have committed the kind of sin that requires a harsh penance, even after it is forgiven. And if your sickness is unto death, your immune system is already weakened and you are quite likely to die anyway. You are on your last legs. In recent history, the "danger of death" came to be applied more leniently, but even so, when the priest arrived at your bedside with bell and stole, he was there as a benevolent harbinger of death, rather than as a joyful messenger of healing and life.

God's ministry of healing had been stood on its head. Life and death were transposed.

We could argue that the changes made between roughly A.D. 400 and 1500 to regulate healing had good reasons lying behind them. But the supreme irony is that for the most part no one expected bodily healing to happen.

This enormous change from "everybody can play" to "only a few can pray," and in limited conditions at that, profoundly influenced the Protestant churches, too, because by the time they appeared on the scene in the sixteenth century, the practice of ordinary people praying for healing had already disappeared. Praying with one another for healing was no longer part of Christian culture.

There were exceptions, a few brave individuals who refused to ignore the cries of the sick begging for personal prayer. One famous exception, St. Bernard (1091–1153), the great reformer of monastic communities and founder of the monastery of Clairvaux, got a reputation as a healer using such traditional and noncontroversial means as making the sign of the cross over the sick person. On one day he is reported to have cured nine blind people, ten who were deaf or dumb and eighteen lame or paralytic. He did this by simply making the sign of the cross over them and they were healed.[4]

His own community and his relatives, however, subscribed to the then-current belief that orthodox Christians were no longer supposed to give the appearance that they were healing the sick:

His uncle Gaudry seems to have been highly suspicious of them [the healings]. More than once he nearly reduced Bernard to tears by telling him that for a man like him to attempt to do miracles was sheer presumption, and that at any rate there was nothing to them.

But one day Gaudry himself fell seriously ill and at once sent for Bernard and begged him to bless and cure him. "Sorry, my dear Uncle," said Bernard smiling, "I fear I can't do that, it would be sheer presumption for me to attempt any such thing." Whereupon Gaudry pleaded that he had only been trying to save his nephew from pride. . . .

In the end Bernard blessed him and cured him both of his illness and of scoffing at his miracles.[5]

Already, during the Middle Ages, the very idea of an ordinary layman praying for the sick had disappeared because healing had become so closely connected with holiness and sanctity. Pilgrimages to shrines were all that was left. And yet the human dimensions of misery and sickness impelled the sick to seek a live person who might pray for them. So when someone with a reputation for holiness appeared on the scene, the sick would beg for any kind of prayer or a touch of the holy person's hand. If someone were healed, the reputed holy person would then attempt to deflect attention somewhere else.

For example, St. John Marie Vianney, the "Curé of Ars," a pastor in nineteenth-century France, attained a great reputation for holiness, and crowds of people tried to reach him. If they were sick and asked for prayer, he would try to deflect attention away from himself by touching them with a relic of St. Philomena. Apparently, many were healed and the Curé would give all the credit to St. Philomena. (By the way, the Catholic Church has removed this early saint, Philomena, from the list of saints, because there is doubt about whether or not she ever really existed!)

For many years then, the shrines, for the most part, offered the only hope for healing for the rank and file of Christians. By the time of the Reformation, however, which began in the sixteenth century and marked the establishment of Protestantism, Catholics still flocked to the shrines of saints to ask for healing. But most Protestant leaders were greatly opposed to such actions. John Calvin, for instance, one of the most influential reformers, regarded devotion to the saints as idolatry. He had huge influence with Reformed Christians with his determination to destroy the ancient healing shrines, which they saw as centers of superstition, as well as fraudulent moneymaking schemes.

Several years ago I visited the magnificent Cathedral of Wells in England. Every saint's statue there had been destroyed by Cromwell's soldiers up to a height of twelve feet—the height a soldier on horseback could reach with his destroying pike—all around the Cathedral's exterior.

In trying to purify religion from any Roman Catholic vestiges, the reformers also rid themselves of healing prayer—and not just in relation to the saints. Calvin also taught "Cessationism," the belief that supernatural healing ended with the death of the last apostle.

It is a belief that still exists in some of the major Protestant denominations. But before we move into the modern era, we have one more transitional period to explore.

16

THE ROYAL TOUCH

And now we come to perhaps the most unusual revelation in our mystery of who nearly killed the healing ministry. It is this: "the Royal Touch," an ancient English and French belief that their kings and queens had the power to heal.[1] As they saw it in those days, the monarch's healing gift did not depend on his or her virtue but came from his position, a divine anointing.

Most English people today (about three out of four in English churches when I have asked for a show of hands) have never even heard about the Royal Touch. And yet, for seven hundred years the English believed that their sovereigns possessed a God-given power to heal those who suffered from the "King's Evil." This was another name for scrofula, a foul disease common in medieval times—a type of tuberculosis infecting the lymph system, creating fetid boils and pustules that broke out on the sick person's body. Scrofula was called the King's Evil because the people believed that the king could heal it through his Royal Touch. The monarchs were healing specialists!

Not to be left behind, the monarchs of France also claimed healing power over scrofula, and in France this belief also lasted for seven hundred years.

Not only did everyone believe in this kind of healing but people acted upon it in a big way; in both France and England, the monarchs regularly held large healing services! It may be hard for us to believe, but King Henry VIII held healing services several times a year.

In England, this healing power was supposed to have dated back to King Edward the Confessor. We definitely know that King Henry I (ca. 1100) touched scrofulous sufferers while making the sign of the cross over them.[2] In one year, Edward I (thirteenth century) blessed some 1,736 people, and many testimonies of healing were recorded.[3] Hard as it may be for us to imagine today, monarchs like Queen Elizabeth I held healing services several times a year, and these were major events.

This healing power was an everyday belief in England and France. Shakespeare, for example, depicts Malcolm fleeing the murderous Macbeth and taking refuge in the court of King Edward the Confessor. There Malcolm witnesses a healing and reports to his companion Macduff that the sick,

> All sworn and ulcerous, pitiful to the eye,
> The mere despair of surgery, he cures,
>   . . . and 'tis spoken,
> To the succeeding royalty he leaves
> The healing benediction.

Macbeth, IV, iii

Contributing to this extraordinary healing phenomenon was the theory that the kings were divinely anointed, and therefore the miracles of healing were signs and wonders that testified to the "divine right of kings." Healing services, consequently, proved that anyone who rebelled against the monarch was fighting God's own appointment.

In this way, healing services served an enormous political purpose. When England was torn by civil war between the houses of Lancaster and York, the rival claimants both claimed to possess the Royal Touch, and they prayed for the sick to prove it.[4] After 1688, the strongly Calvinist kings and queens of England imported from Holland stopped holding healing services. (Perhaps in some way this made it easier for the American colonists to revolt against King George III a century later.)

In both England and France, the monarch would actually touch each sufferer, as well as say a prayer for him or her, in a prescribed healing ritual. If you have ever prayed for individuals at a healing service, you know how much time and energy you expend and how tired you can get. Most healing evangelists today do not pray for each and every individual in a crowd, and yet the English and French monarchs did. It gives us an idea of the expenditure of effort these monarchs put out, and what importance they placed upon their healing ministry! Each healing service took the better part of two or three entire days.

To take one example, King Louis XIV of France prayed for three thousand scrofulous people on Pentecost Sunday 1698.[5] (Again, it is hard for us to believe that someone like Louis XIV would take time out from his sumptuous court at Versailles in order to spend so much time praying for the sick). In England, Charles II (who also presided over a profligate court) prayed for 23,000 people in a four-year span and for some 100,000 in his 25-year reign.[6]

As mentioned above, theologians taught that healing came through the king's divinely appointed office, not his personal holiness; they believed that kings belonged to a higher state than laypeople. Some theologians even taught that a king's consecration was equal in spiritual power to that of a bishop.

When we consider that scrofula was a foul-smelling disease featuring oozing pustules, as well as realizing how tiring and difficult these healing ceremonies must have been, we can see how important healing services were to kings and people alike. Especially impressive is the fact that the French king stood throughout the ceremony (the English monarchs sat) and touched each person, while praying (translated from French):

> The King toucheth thee,
> and God healeth thee.[7]

Thousands of people flocked to these healing services, and apparently many were cured, some dramatically. The basic idea was Christian, namely, that God was the power behind the healing, while the monarch was only a secondary human mediator. But, as has been the case for hundreds of years, healing was facing newer and more severe limitations.

Eventually, the kings became so protective of their privilege that Charles I of England (1650) decided to put the traditional folk healers out of business. In England, as in many other cultures, there was a traditional folk belief that the seventh son (in a family with seven sons and no intervening daughters) was a born healer. The seventh son of a seventh son was supposed to be an even more potent healer. (This is still a common belief in many countries and in some locales in the United States, such as Appalachia and Louisiana.) Because some English scrofula patients were turning to seventh sons in preference to coming to the king's healing services, King Charles actually made it a crime—a crime of lèse-majesté—for seventh sons to exercise their traditional healing ministry.[8]

The royal healing ministries continued strongly in England, until the influence of Calvinism finally put a stop to it in 1688.[9] For a hundred and fifty years previous to that, Protestant advisors tried to influence the monarchs to stamp out these healing services, but the kings and queens (such as Elisabeth I and Edward VI)[10] continued on because it was so popular with the people. Besides, the Royal Touch emphasized their divine authority. The monarchs were not about to give up such power!

In France the healing services did not stop until the French Revolution, when Louis XVI had his head chopped off by the guillotine. In the nineteenth century, the French kings returned to power and tried to resurrect their healing services, but due to the triumph of secularism, the services no longer appealed to the populace. King Charles X of France conducted the last royal healing service on May 31, 1825.

As part of this fascinating story, we should note another fascinating irony:

- In England it was *zealous religious reformers* who persuaded the monarchs to stop praying for the sick. So great were the political benefits that it took a hundred and fifty years from the time Protestant monarchs took over until they finally stopped.
- In France it was the *atheistic reformers*, who worshiped the Goddess of Reason, who instantly stopped royal healing services by lopping off the king's head.

This era represented the strictest narrowing of the healing ministry. In all of England, only one person could pray for healing! And the same in France. Political advantage kept that one royal person in the healing business. And no one objected! Where were the bishops, the priests and ministers? Apparently, they were no longer rivals in the business of praying for the sick.

Gradually, as we have seen, even the monarchs stopped praying for the sick. Oddly enough, politics had kept it alive. And now we will see how the religious reformers did everything they could to cut even that slim thread.

17

THE PROTESTANT REFORMATION AND THE FURTHER DECLINE OF HEALING

The fervent cry of the Protestant reformers was faithfulness to Scripture, along with getting rid of all false traditions that obscure true religion. We would expect, then, that they would return to the beliefs of apostolic days and restore the scriptural practices of healing prayer and exorcism. Ironically, the very reverse happened; the great reformers had no interest in giving life to the Kingdom message that Jesus had stressed so passionately.

Martin Luther

Martin Luther, the German Reformation leader, did not tackle any questions connected with healing; he simply passed on what he had learned about that neglected subject. But when his friend Melanchthon fell grievously ill, he prayed and, to his delight, Melanchthon was healed.

139

As we read about Luther's life, it seems apparent that his great worry of having sinned, his great fear of his father and his great terror about the judgment of God might well have been helped if he had known about prayer for healing. Nevertheless, his important discoveries about God's mercy and grace should prepare Lutherans to understand the Good News about God's healing power with openness and gladness.

John Calvin

The reformer who most deeply wounded the healing ministry was the most influential of all the theologians of the Reformation, John Calvin (1509–64). When we find that Baptists today, for instance, have great devotion to the Bible but do not believe in a healing ministry or in deliverance, the reason ultimately goes back to Calvin's teaching—even though they may have no idea that this is so.

Although Catholics retained a belief in the miraculous, they nevertheless had come to view some aspects of religion intellectually. As we have said, they tended to emphasize that God healed in order to prove something, either that Jesus was the Son of God, or that the Roman Catholic Church was the One True Church, or that a particular individual was a saint. Somehow, the idea that Jesus healed primarily because of His compassion and love was obscured.

It is in relation to compassion, actually, that Catholics often approach Jesus' mother, Mary, and pray for her intercession. Catholics resisted Cessationism and retained their belief in the miraculous, but their faith expectancy had faded—and only an occasional healing occurred.

Calvin chose Augustine as his favorite theologian from early Christianity, but he did not pick up on Augustine's admission (in his book of *Retractions*) that he had been wrong in teaching that healing was rare. Instead, Calvin carried the teaching of the early Augustine to a further extreme. For Calvin, miracles were not just rare: They ended with the death of the last apostle. He believed in every miracle described in the New Testament, but after that, it was over. He converted Cessationism into a basic doctrine.

He further taught that demons had been banished from this world after the Resurrection; so, in addition to calling for the abolition of the healing ministry, he also did away with exorcism and deliverance, at least for Christians. Calvin left no doubt in his teaching that healing through prayer was dead and gone.

> But that gift of healing, like the rest of the miracles, which the Lord willed to be brought forth for a time, has vanished away in order to make the new preaching of the gospel marvelous forever. Therefore, even if we grant to the full that anointing was a sacrament . . . it has nothing to do with us, to whom the administering of such powers has not been committed.[1]

How ironic that healing and deliverance, so central to Jesus' preaching, were totally done away with by the Protestant Reformation in the name of making "the new preaching of the Gospel marvelous forever." The very ones who were most devoted to the Word of God and championed its literal interpretation came to believe that God meant healing to last only for those early apostolic days.

How did Calvin come to such a negative conclusion that has continued to influence his followers for centuries afterward (Presbyterians, Baptists, and most other evangelicals, to some extent)?

We can be sympathetic to Calvin's position when we realize that the only healing ministry that he actually saw practiced in the Europe of the sixteenth century was connected to real abuses. In those days healing in the Catholic Church was confined mainly to three activities, and we will look at each of these:

- pilgrimages to healing shrines
- the Sacrament of Anointing
- the Royal Touch

Pilgrimages to Healing Shrines

As we have said, the healing ministry was kept alive for hundreds of years by pilgrimages to healing shrines. That was the good part. At the same time, the pilgrimages could be criticized for the same reason that indulgences came under attack.

These popular shrines featured vast collections of relics, numbering in the thousands, filling up churches and chapels and bringing in enormous revenues from the pilgrims' contributions. Like the promotion of indulgences, these shrines gave the appearance of being huge money-making schemes. And we have to note that just as many educated people today question the ministry of "faith-healers" because of their approach to fund-raising, which often seems to take advantage of the simple faith of ordinary Christians. Calvin and the other reformers decided that the healing shrines savored more of greed than of faith. "Get rid of these shrines!" was their natural response to what they saw as superstition.

In addition, they believed that devotion to the saints detracted from the worship of Jesus Christ. Mary, the mother of Jesus, seemed, in popular religion, to have become more important than Jesus, and she with the saints seemed to have become the principal mediators between God and human beings.

Although this was not authentic Catholic teaching, in practice it seemed that more attention was paid to the saints than to Jesus. As a result, Calvinists, such as Cromwell's troops in England, smashed stained-glass windows and priceless statues in the churches of England and the Continent. The Calvinists had absolutely no regrets about destroying some of the great artistic achievements of the Middle Ages; in their minds, they were following the scriptural injunction against idolatry and preventing Christians in the future from falling prey to it.

The Sacrament of Anointing

As for the Sacrament of Anointing, or Extreme Unction, Calvin also poured out his scorn upon this rite, because the Catholic Church waited until the sick were nearly dead before the priests could minister it. You can sense the anger in his words when he describes how priests

smear with their grease not the sick but half-dead corpses when they are already drawing their last breath, or (as they say) "in extremis." If in their sacrament they have a powerful medicine with which to alleviate the agony of diseases, . . . it is cruel of them never to heal in time. James would have the sick man anointed by the elders of the church; these men allow only a priestling as anointer.[2]

In ridiculing the Catholic Sacrament of Extreme Unction as a useless, manmade ritual, he was also assuming that Cessationism was true. And thus he "doomed Protestantism to a long period of healing powerlessness."[3] It took four hundred years before the Roman Catholic Church recognized the validity of Calvin's criticisms and restored this sacrament to its primary purpose of healing the sick.

The Royal Touch

It certainly did not help that one of the last remaining healing ministries in Calvin's time was that of the monarchs of France and England. The dissolute Bourbon kings in the profligate court of Versailles would hardly have inspired the strict Calvinists to a lively belief in healing, although thousands came to the kings' annual royal healing services. In fact, it was the Calvinist monarch William of Orange, whom the English brought over from Holland to assume the English throne in 1688, who stopped the seven-hundred-year-old tradition of kings praying for the sick. He saw nothing but superstition in the healing rite and, consequently, when he was asked to pray, he resolutely refused to touch the sick.

Nevertheless, a few years later, when Queen Anne came to power, she realized the great advantages (including political) of praying for scrofula sufferers. She resurrected the royal healing rites and prayed for the sick until shortly before her death in 1714. After this, the English invited the German House of Hanover to cross the Channel and assume the throne of Great Britain in 1714, and these German Protestants never again tried to resurrect the Royal Touch. It took nearly two hundred years from the time the Protestants took over rule in England for Calvin's influence to finally end the royal healing services in England.

France, remaining a Catholic country until the French Revolution, kept the tradition of royal healing services alive until later, when the guillotine chopped off the head of Louis XVI (1789). Fascinating to note, though, that the last two Bourbon kings, Louis XV and Louis XVI, were not as ardent in praying for the sick as had been their predecessors. One reason was that Catholics expected the king to be free of serious sin before performing a religious ceremony, and Louis XV wasn't eager to confess his sins.

For several years, therefore, he cancelled healing services because dalliances with his mistresses were so well known. As critics quipped, he practiced the Royal Touch upon his favorite mistress. The influence of Voltaire and a scoffing Enlightenment mentality had made the nobility skeptical about divine healing, although the ordinary people still eagerly sought prayer. As a result of these educated doubts, the second verse of the royal prayer was changed from "God heals thee" (*Dieu te guérit*) to "May God heal thee" (*Dieu te guérisse*).

In Reformed theology the other charisms, including such spiritual experiences as visions, tongues or prophecy, came to be seen as delusions. The only spiritual experience that Calvin accepted was the salvation experience and enlightenment while reading Scripture. Augustine's abandonment of the charismatic gifts listed by Paul in favor of Isaiah's seven gifts was now bearing its ultimate fruit.

Calvin bought into the idea that Augustine had originally taught: Miracles primarily point to true doctrine, rather than showing us how much Jesus loves us. Faith as "expectancy" had become faith as "belief in solid doctrine." The verse "Blessed are those who have not seen and yet have believed" (John 20:29) was taken to mean that having faith based on actually seeing healing take place was an inferior brand of faith. He did not take literally the scriptural passage "And these signs will accompany those who believe . . . they will place their hands on sick people, and they will get well" (Mark 16:17–18), which connects faith with healing.

Anyone who has prayed with the sick knows that healing prayer is a risk requiring faith, because the prayer comes *before* any actual evidence, before any actual healing takes place. Rather than being an inferior kind of faith, I think, actually, that it is stronger. Still, Christianity had come to concentrate upon the intellect, rather than upon the heart, as the main motive for healing.

18

THE ENLIGHTENMENT
AND DISPENSATIONALISM

The Final Blows

Although Calvin shut down the healing ministry in Protestantism because of his disdain for Catholic practices, he maintained an absolute belief in the literal truth of the biblical account of miracles. It took another two hundred years before these healing miracles of Jesus and His disciples were called into question.

Perhaps the most influential philosopher in the Enlightenment, a movement of the eighteenth century with an emphasis on rationalism, was David Hume, who flat out declared that the miracles in the life of Jesus never happened. If no miracles are happening in the present, why should we believe that they ever took place in the past? Hume (1711–1776) was a Scottish philosopher who was the leading exponent of the school of Scottish Realism. Science and religion had been gradually growing apart since the Middle Ages, when most outstanding scientists were clerics (such as St. Albert the Great, ca. 1200–1280, the most renowned scientist of his day and the mentor of St. Thomas Aquinas).

But now in the eighteenth century, the intellectual atmosphere of Europe had so drastically changed that the findings of science and religion were often seen as opposed to each other. Galileo's famous trial, in which church authorities maintained fiercely that the Bible taught that the sun moved around the earth, was now two centuries past, and, increasingly, educated Europeans were skeptical of the claims of a church that had lost credibility in their eyes. Scientific materialism taught that if you couldn't see it, if you couldn't measure it, you couldn't say for certain that it existed. Angels and demons remained embedded in popular belief, as did miraculous healing, but they were no longer part of the belief system of the educated classes.

David Hume wrote the influential *An Enquiry Concerning Human Understanding*, which banished any remaining belief in miracles from European secular thought. The liberal wing of Protestants no longer tried to defend the historicity of the gospels but developed the theory that the miracles were "myths." They regarded the New Testament accounts of healing and exorcism as stories that were true in the sense that they represented not literal, physical truths, but a spiritual meaning deeper than any purely literal understanding.

For example, the healing of a leper in Scripture stood for the healing of his spiritual leprosy—sin—rather than a supernatural healing of a physical disease. The multiplication of the loaves and fishes was not an extraordinary physical increase in bread and fishes; it probably recalled a spiritual event in which the multitude were so deeply inspired by Jesus that they gave away the excess food they had previously hidden away in their loose-flowing garments. In this way, everyone was fed—a miracle of love, which was an even greater miracle than a physical multiplication of loaves.

There were still some Protestant defenders of Jesus' miracles, but they did not believe that miracles continue to take place in our times. These defenders of the literal historicity of the gospels became the conservative wing of the evangelicals, but they held on to Cessationism.

These two wings of Protestantism—the "conservatives" who believed that miracles ceased nineteen hundred years ago, and the "liberals" who believed that they never happened at all—still represent major divisions among Protestant Christians and affect us in our own day.

The effects of a secular, scientific worldview have particularly influenced the educated, who have come to see healing and exorcism as the remnants of a primitive understanding of nature (and religion) in which intelligent people can no longer believe. Once again, we find "ordinary" Christians, those not highly educated, who still believe in a literal understanding of the New Testament stories, while the professors and ministers see things very differently.

Take, for example, the Scottish theologian and popular author of New Testament studies, William Barclay, who wrote *The Daily Study Bible Series*. You will find Barclay in almost every Christian bookstore, lining the Scripture bookshelf section. Barclay stated that he was delighted to be a "theological middleman" who always had one aim—to convey the results of scholarship to the ordinary reader and to help people "know Jesus Christ more clearly, to love him more dearly, and to follow him more nearly."[1]

Since Barclay is a popular, commonly accepted author, it is significant that most of his readers are apparently not disturbed when he implies that Jesus simply used the power of suggestion when He cast out evil spirits. In his commentary on freeing the man possessed by a mute and deaf spirit (Matthew 12:22–29), for instance, Barclay makes this statement as self-evident:

> In the eastern world it was not only mental and psychological illness which was ascribed to the influence of demons and devils; all illness was ascribed to their malignant power. Exorcism was therefore very commonly practiced; and was in fact frequently completely effective.
>
> There is nothing in that to be surprised at. When people believe in demon-possession, it is easy to convince themselves that they are so possessed; when they come under that delusion, the symptoms of demon-possession immediately arise. Even amongst ourselves anyone can think himself into having a headache, or can convince himself that he has the symptoms of an illness. When a person under such a delusion was confronted with an exorcist in whom he had confidence, often the delusion was dispelled and a cure resulted. In such cases if a man was convinced he was cured, he was cured.[2]

Notice that Barclay uses the word *delusion* three times.

The next logical question for us to ask is, Was Jesus Himself deluded? But I think Barclay realized that question would be going too far and does not consider it.

John Nelson Darby

A combination of Calvin's Cessationism, Scottish Realism and de-mythologizing Scripture had taken a heavy toll on the practice of praying for the sick. Then, along came John Nelson Darby (1800–1882), who further damaged the healing ministry, coming at it from another direction.

Up to now we have described only a few from the bewildering variety of Christian leaders who rose to prominence over the centuries and then disappeared like comets. But some have had a lasting effect upon us—and upon the healing ministry—such as Augustine and Calvin. We would hardly need to mention Darby, except that his teachings have had a lasting effect for two hundred years, even upon many evangelicals who might not even recognize his name.

Darby was a strong leader who joined the newly formed Plymouth Brethren—founded by a dentist in the 1830s in reaction to the sad condition of Anglicanism in England and Ireland. The Brethren desired to return to the simplicity of the Gospel and wanted to move out of church buildings in order to build loving communities in small households. They viewed the class divisions in English society as contrary to Gospel values, and in their leveling process they scorned ordination and celebrated the Lord's Supper in their households.

John Darby joined the Plymouth Brethren in Dublin after he had been through a disillusioning experience in an Anglican seminary; he had been shocked to learn how the Anglicans were trying to force conversion upon impoverished Catholics. He dropped Anglicanism to adopt Calvin's teachings and soon became the Brethren's most influential theologian. He was such a gifted leader that by the time he died he had founded more than a thousand Brethren churches.

He studied the Bible intensely and came up with a number of theories that have profoundly influenced the conservative wing of evangelical Christianity. His most influential theological innovation was Dispensationalism, a theory that claims that Church history is divided into several eras or "dispensations."

For Darby, the Gospel era was a separate dispensation from our own time, and healing and the other charismatic gifts (in 1 Corinthians 12) were intended only for the special dispensation of apostolic times. Like Calvin, Darby believed that healing and the other charismatic gifts ended with the death of the last apostle. Ironically, there was an explosion of these charismatic gifts in England during these years among the Irvingites, a Pentecostal group who claimed to exercise all the gifts. Unfortunately, the Irvingites also exhibited some excesses and were branded as heretics—not only by Darby but by most English Christians of that day and they had no lasting influence.

Darby emphasized a number of teachings that were regarded in his day as unorthodox but are now accepted by many evangelicals. These teachings include an emphasis upon the closeness of the End Times and the Great Tribulation, during which apostate Christians and nonbelievers will be left behind to suffer while the true believers are taken up to heaven (the Rapture); and the belief that before the Second Coming, the Jewish people are to reclaim Jerusalem and the Holy Land. On an interesting note, the extremely popular *Left Behind* series of books, imaginatively describing the End Times, have sold in the millions, and they ultimately owe their inspiration to Darby.

He was so convinced of the imminent end of the world that he predicted it would come in 1842. Then, like so many other Christian "prophets" over the course of history, he continued to teach with great authority for another forty years, even when the world did not go up in flames. Increasingly, Darby became more authoritarian in his views and he expelled several leaders, famous in his day, from the Brethren—notably Watchman Nee and George Müller.

Another of Darby's legacies to today's evangelicals is that, because he was convinced that the end of the world was coming almost immediately, he taught that true Christians should come out from the world and forget about taking any action to transform it. Social action seemed a waste of time when he considered the urgency of getting people saved. He saw both the world and the Church as lost and doomed to destruction. Even in our day, you can still hear some evangelicals say, "Social justice is just rearranging the furniture on the deck of the Titanic. The ship is sinking. Don't waste your time!"

Before Darby, evangelicals were not only concerned about preaching conversion but they also were immersed in social issues. They saw the transformation of individuals and of the world as part of one Gospel vision. Charles Finney, for example, the Billy Graham of his day, was a major figure who worked toward the abolition of slavery shortly before the Civil War. (Finney had a personal transforming encounter with the Holy Spirit, leading him to become the first "professional" evangelist in America. His preaching ushered in the "Second Great Awakening" in American history in the mid-1800s.)

William Wilberforce was an equally strong voice in Britain. In fact, the abolitionist cause was so identified with the strong evangelical move of the mid-1800s that the Roman Catholic archbishop of New York excoriated the abolition movement as a brainchild of Protestantism.

But after Darby, Protestants were further divided into two wings: those who stressed crusades, revivals and "getting people saved," and those considered "liberals" (such as the World Council of Churches) who concentrated on social justice. Very few churches emphasized both. Instead of remaining a single group of Christians with a double emphasis, they instead became two opposing groups who were often suspicious of the other's vision and orthodoxy.[3]

I remember finding this very response when I gave several dozen retreats in Latin America in the 1970s. My topic was usually the power of the Holy Spirit—especially as shown in healing. Most of these dedicated Catholic missionaries—priests and nuns—were strongly identified with the poor and were working for greater social justice.

Initially, they were prejudiced against what I was saying because they associated it with topics emphasized by some North American televangelists who stressed the "health and wealth" gospel. It always took several days to convince the missionaries that I was not preaching a gospel that was too comfortable to be real. But many of them eventually put the double emphasis of the baptism with the Spirit and social justice together in one vision.

Particularly in Bolivia, several missionaries understood the vision of combining the message of the Church's preferential option for the poor, together with the need for the power of the Spirit. In one instance, a group of missionaries was warned in prayer that the military were going to plant false evidence of revolutionary activity in their living quarters. Warned by the vision, they were able to avoid the plot that would have resulted in their falsely being arrested and shipped out of Bolivia.

Darby didn't have a huge influence in England but he made half a dozen visits to the United States and converted several key leaders to his way of interpreting Scripture. Notable among these were Dwight L.

Moody, the great evangelist and founder of Wheaton College, and C. I. Scofield, who was editor of the extraordinarily influential Scofield Reference Bible. Scofield's footnotes repeated Darby's Dispensationalism and were read by a multitude of Scripture students who seemed to assume that what was in the footnotes was the inspired understanding of the biblical text.

As a result, Darby's teaching that the charisms are dead in our day reinforced Calvin's Cessationism, thereby shutting out healing prayer from the conservative evangelical wing of Protestants. The more liberal wing of Protestants was influenced by the teaching of Rudolf Bultmann, and they did not believe that healings had ever really taken place, even during the life of Jesus.

In this paradoxical way, both conservative and liberal Protestants shut the door on healing prayer and exorcism. Among Catholics, belief in healing remained among the people who went on pilgrimages to shrines to seek it. But it was regarded as rare, and ordinary Catholics no longer believed with any expectancy that they themselves could pray for healing.

By the end of the 1800s, only the slightest flickering pulse of life was detectable in the ministry of Christian healing.

Rudolf Bultmann

Even closer to our time, Rudolf Bultmann (1884–1976) continued the liberal tradition of regarding the miracle stories of the gospels as "myths." He was the single most influential New Testament scholar of the twentieth century.[4] As a critical historian, Bultmann assumed that the world was a closed system in which God had no influence: The healing miracles were impossible and the Resurrection did not happen in any literal sense. All these were myths, no longer believable in the modern age. (*Demythologizing* is the term most often used in referring to Bultmann's thought.) Although his form-criticism of the New Testament has much to offer, his teaching can give the impression summed up by the words of a student who attended a lecture on the gospels. When I asked the student what he had learned about the New Testament, he replied, "It isn't true."

While this response oversimplifies what Bultmann taught, it still represents a typical reaction of the ordinary Christian, who comes away with the impression that the whole study of the Bible is so complicated that only professional theologians are equipped to understand it.

Many prominent professors at German universities were Bultmann's students and his writings still have a great impact. Since his followers have taken over control of many Protestant seminaries (not those run by conservative evangelicals) his teaching has influenced numerous preachers. I would say that, in a way, seminaries are run by genteel scholars, once typified by the "God is dead" theology in the 1960s and the "post-Christian" era in Europe. As a result, his school of theology, going well beyond Cessationism, has influenced most educated Protestants, most especially the clergy, who would never consider praying for healing or casting out demons. Once, when asked about Johann Christophe Blumhardt, the Lutheran pastor who rediscovered healing and deliverance, Bultmann scoffed at his ministry as a "legend" and an "abomination" to Protestantism.[5]

Regardless of which of these many theories we accept, it seems only logical to conclude that questioning the reality of Jesus' healing ministry will lead inevitably to questioning the greatest miracle of them all, His Resurrection from the dead. Indeed, this is happening today; a major scholarly battle is being waged at the core of Christianity regarding the life, death and resurrection of Jesus.

What began slowly back in the fifth century, doubting God's willingness to heal, has eventually led us to the "search for the historical Jesus" and to the "Jesus Seminars," where scholars vote on Jesus' sayings and actions in the gospels, deciding whether or not He actually made certain statements, and whether or not He actually performed certain healing miracles. And why not judge that the greatest miracle of all, Jesus' resurrection, is even more impossible?

Healing is now all but dead.

Case closed.

PART 4

THE LONG
ROAD BACK

19

EXPECTANT FAITH REMAINS
IN THE PEOPLE

We have now seen how many factors nearly smothered healing prayer, even though it was part of the essence of Christianity. Ironically, it was the very factors in Christian life that you would expect to keep it alive that mysteriously nearly killed it:

The religious leaders, the bishops and priests, were doing very little to promote healing.

Ordinary Christians no longer were encouraged or taught how to pray for healing.

The ones who later came to reform the Church condemned the practice of healing as "papist superstition."

And yet it survived.

How?

It was "the little people"—the sick, the harassed and those who wandered "like sheep without a shepherd"—who kept it alive.

They were the ones who needed it. They kept searching. And hoping. Looking for someone who could offer God's healing.

Crowds of people wanted someone to pray for them. And hardly anyone was around to do the praying.

Now that we have described how it was that Christians lost their confidence to pray for healing as an ordinary part of life, we can balance that bleak history with a glorious testimony about the faith that remained. In this chapter we will go back and scan the centuries. In the next chapter we will view the lives of individuals who pursued healing, and then in following chapters focus on movements that made it work.

This story of restoration begins in the Middle Ages. It is humbling to realize that the belief in the miraculous element in Christianity burned more brightly then than it does today, when now the very words *miraculous* and *supernatural* are out of fashion among theologians in most of the established Christian churches. In fact, theologians today might consider most of the stories we read in the lives of the saints of the Middle Ages as mere legend and superstition.

We read, for example, how St. Patrick (ca. 389–461) converted Ireland through an extraordinary series of spiritual power confrontations with the druid priests, much like Elijah's power contest with the 450 prophets of Baal (see 1 Kings 18).

Patrick's journeys all began when he heard a voice that continually guided him over the years to his mission in Ireland, much as St. Paul had been guided to Macedonia. When he arrived in Ireland, Patrick realized that he needed to convert the pagan king Laoghaire at his headquarters in Tara. The druid priests were infuriated and, in that violent time, they tried to kill Patrick and his companions. In an extraordinary succession of adventures, Patrick escaped these attempts to kill him, such as when he passed by a group of assassins, unharmed, because he had become invisible. (When his little group escaped, they composed the famous "Breastplate of Patrick" prayer.)

Later at a banquet at Tara, Patrick and his five companions astonished the king by suddenly appearing at table after passing through locked doors. After the king invited Patrick to sit next to him, the chief druid laced Patrick's drink with poison. Patrick made the sign of the cross over the cup and his beverage froze, except for the drop of poison. Patrick proceeded to pour the poisoned drop out onto the table. Then, after he blessed his cup, he drank the potion without dying.

This encounter was followed by other tests: Patrick made snow disappear, turned darkness on a plain into light and, last of all, conquered the druids in a trial by fire in which one druid was placed in a wooden hut while one of Patrick's followers, covered by Patrick's cloak, was placed in a second hut built of dried out wood (the druid's hut was freshly cut). Both huts were torched and Patrick's follower emerged unharmed, and Patrick's cloak was not even singed.

This dramatic power encounter still wasn't enough to convert the king, but it did impress him enough to give Patrick permission to preach. As a result, within a few years Patrick had baptized tens of thousands and built hundreds of churches. By the time of his death, Ireland had mostly abandoned the druid religion and had become Christian.[1]

Patrick's story took place only about one hundred years after Constantine's conversion. In it we still see the extraordinary belief in God's working signs and wonders to authenticate the preaching of the Gospel. While we can question the historic witness—some stories may have grown into legend—we still see a wildly expectant faith.

Eight hundred years later, Christians still believed that God spoke directly through dreams. St. Dominic, for example, had determined to found his community, the Order of Preachers (1215). Pope Innocent III was reluctant to give Dominic permission, but the pope had a dream in which he saw Dominic holding up the Basilica of St. John Lateran,[2] which was collapsing. The dream was enough to change the pope's mind and led to the founding of the Dominican Order,[3] which, since then, has survived for nearly eight hundred years.

Dominic also raised a young man from the dead. The young man, named Napoleon, was killed in Rome when he fell off a horse. Dominic had the body carried into a chapel and there, in the presence of three cardinals and numbers of priests and nuns, he blessed the corpse and shouted, "Napoleon, in the name of our Lord Jesus Christ, arise." Immediately, in the presence of these reliable witnesses, the young man arose, whole and well.[4]

Now, Dominic lived nearly a thousand years after Constantine's conversion, so stories like this show that Christian leaders still readily accepted the possibility of God's extraordinary gifts of guidance and healing. And an occasional leader, like Dominic, would go counter to custom and not only heal the sick, but raise the dead.

One hundred years later, one of Dominic's followers, St. Vincent Ferrer (1350–1419), was not embarrassed to estimate that he had worked three thousand miracles and, of these, 873 were documented by the Church when he was canonized! He was one of the few Christian leaders in the fifteen hundred years following Augustine who would still purposely pray for healing. He got off to a good start, for when he was still in his mother's womb, a blind woman reportedly touched her head against his mother's stomach and was instantly healed.

Vincent became perhaps the greatest preacher of his age, speaking to crowds numbering in the thousands and being heard distinctly by every individual. Large groups of followers would travel with him from city to city. His extraordinary preaching success sounds very much like the Great Awakening four hundred years later, when George Whitefield preached throughout the eastern colonies in what later became the United States.

Many of the stories from the lives of the saints strain credulity because there is no natural explanation for them. We also know that the people in those days were not as concerned as we are about scientific evidence. It is like the story of the three Indians and their miraculous filling of teeth that I narrated in my book, *Healing*.[5] The story was so incredible that several foreign publishers left it out of their translations.

The point about these stories is not that we necessarily need to believe them but, at the least, they demonstrate that some Christians, even some leaders, a thousand years after Augustine, remained full of expectant faith and still believed in the possibility of remarkable supernatural events. The history of the Catholic saints is filled with fascinating stories of the miraculous. You have probably read something about the life of Francis of Assisi (1181–1226), who heard Jesus speak from the cross and who healed a leper upon embracing him. And then we all have heard the story of how Francis preached to the birds.[6]

St. Catherine of Siena (1347–1380) not only healed the sick but also had the extraordinary gift of looking into people's souls and confronting them with their secret sins. She used this gift of discernment boldly to confront Pope Urban VI and get him to leave Avignon, France, where for seventy years the popes had established their headquarters. She persuaded him to move the papacy back to Rome and end the scandalous division in the Church (at one time three men claimed to be pope).[7]

And then we all have read about Joan of Arc (1412–1431) and how she claimed that St. Michael had appeared to her and guided her to meet the French Dauphin and lead his army to win back France from the English.[8]

St. Martin De Porres (1579–1639) from Lima, Peru, is said to have walked through closed doors, and his very touch had the power to heal. Since he took care of the sick in his own Dominican community, he tried to hide his healing gift under the cover of bandaging wounds and giving the sick herbal remedies, but the people saw through it all and realized that God had blessed Martin with an extraordinary healing gift.[9]

Even after the period of the scientific Enlightenment, when so many theologians began to question the possibility of the miraculous, the ordinary people maintained a strong belief in the extraordinary power of God that goes beyond human powers. Even during the Renaissance, we still read about holy people whose lives were characterized by extraordinary gifts of the Spirit. St. Francis Xavier (1506–1552), the celebrated Jesuit missionary, was traveling in India when he heard of a woman who was dying in childbirth. Sorcerers were treating her with their incantations. He went to her and spoke so convincingly about Jesus Christ that she was converted. And when Francis baptized her, she was healed and gave birth to a healthy baby.[10]

Even in the skeptical nineteenth century, St. John Bosco (1815–1888) worked remarkable miracles. In 1866, when Don Bosco was building a big church in Turin, Italy, he regularly ran out of money. One day he needed four thousand francs to pay his contractors and, during the morning one benefactor gave him one thousand francs. So that afternoon, he went wandering through the streets, seeking a miracle for the other three thousand. A wealthy man's servant met up with him and asked him to visit his master, who had been laid up in bed for three years. Seizing the chance, John went to see the sick man.

"Father," the man said, "I need your prayers. I hurt so much that I can't move at all, and the doctors give me no hope. If I get even a little relief, I'll make a generous donation to your work."

"How fortunate!" said Don Bosco. "Today we need three thousand francs . . ."

"I couldn't possibly arrange that today. . . . Besides, I'm too sick to go to the bank."

"And why shouldn't you get up and go to the bank?" asked Don Bosco. "We need the money now. Nothing is impossible to God."

Then he rounded up everyone in the house to pray for the man's healing.

With the whole household around him as witnesses, the man recovered instantaneously. He jumped out of bed and asked for his clothes.[11]

A very Italian part of the story is that he immediately ordered a big meal. And then, after dinner, he walked down to the bank and drew out the three thousand francs, which he delightedly gave to Don Bosco.

This kind of popular enthusiasm for the miraculous continues into this century in the remarkable life of Padre Pio—St. Padre Pio of Pietrelcina (1887–1968), who is reported to have worked thousands of miracles in our own time. Padre Pio was a Capuchin Franciscan and, like Francis of Assisi, told the astonishing story of how an angel imprinted on his hands, feet and side the wounds of Jesus. "I felt as if I was dying," he said. "When the mysterious creature left, I found that my hands, feet, and side had been pierced and were bleeding. . . . The wound in my heart bleeds continuously, especially from Thursday evening until Saturday."[12]

Padre Pio was especially famous for being able to sense what was going on in the depths of people's hearts—what charismatics would term the "word of knowledge"—which would often lead to deep repentance and conversion. Thousands of pilgrims went to his little Italian town of San Giovanni Rotondo, outside Rome. I often meet people who made trips to Italy to see him. One great admirer was Pope John Paul II, who sped up the ordinary process of his canonization to have Padre Pio named a saint.

These examples from the Catholic tradition show us how the desire of the laypeople for healing, particularly when they were no longer allowed to pray, more or less drew leaders into the healing ministry.

In fact, the priests were sometimes ensnared into praying for healing. People would sense that a particular priest was truly a holy man, so they would ask him to do something in the line of his regular duty. For example, they would ask him to bless them—an ordinary activity. Then, after the blessing, the sick would discover that they had been healed. If it happened often enough, people took notice and recognized these individuals as healers, whether they wanted to pray for healing or not. They were accidental healers, as it were. Only a few, such as Vincent Ferrer and Don Bosco, were bold enough to actually pray for healing and not feel embarrassed by their gift.

A typical example of this "accidental" healer was St. Salvator of Orta (1520–1567). As a lay brother of the Franciscan friary[13] of Tortosa, Spain, he was assigned to beg alms for his community. While begging, he met sick people who asked for him to pray. When he simply made the sign of the cross over them, many found they were healed. This created his reputation as a miracle worker and multitudes flocked to his friary.

The crowds became so overwhelming that Brother Salvator was secretly transferred to another friary, near Orta. But the people soon found out that he had been moved and flocked to Orta. Among those healed was a ten-year-old girl, blind from birth. This healing took place while Salvator was praying with her parents before an image of the Madonna and Child. When the girl exclaimed, "How beautiful is the little child whom our Lady carries in her arms!" they realized that, for the first time, the girl was able to see.[14]

Unfortunately, the ancient stories about the saints—such as about how St. George killed the dragon—contained many legendary elements. In recent years, the Roman Catholic Church has had to sort out what was credible from what seemed to be the result of overeager imaginations. Some favorite saints (such as St. Christopher and St. George) have even been removed from the calendar of saints, much to the dismay of many devout souls who had little statues and medals dedicated to these patrons of travel, or even of entire countries (George, for instance, was the patron of England).

This necessary sorting out in a scientific age between fact and legend has resulted in some confusion: What can we believe in anymore? In the Roman Catholic Church this contributes in our day to a division between two streams of spirituality. One is a popular stream in which a traditional belief in the intercession of the saints and the miraculous continues on. The other includes theologians and educated Catholics who question whether or not such phenomena as "supernatural" healing and an active demonic realm are still believable in our day. Both groups live on, in parallel streams, without condemnation. In fact, some six thousand shrines still exist in Europe with Church approval, even while a popular French Catholic spiritual author some forty years ago wrote, "Miracles are merely a holdover from the age of pre-scientific explanation, an anachronism."[15] In contrast, six million pilgrims a year go to the healing shrine of Lourdes in the Pyrenees mountains of France.

I find it interesting that charismatic Protestant teachers who have spoken to all kinds of Christian groups have often told me that, to their surprise, Catholics seem to be more open to healing prayer and the other charismatic gifts—even praying in tongues—than are many evangelicals. I believe that this is because of the long-enduring belief in healing by the laypeople over the centuries.

I remember back, sometime around 1970, I was trying to explain to a high-ranking priest why so many nuns were taking the bus to Pittsburgh to attend Kathryn Kuhlmann's healing services.[16] He gave as his opinion that her ministry was fake and that she probably hired shills to take the microphone and act as if they had been healed. I then noted that a personal friend of mine had gone to one of Kathryn's services and been healed of a deviated septum.

By the seventeenth century, the effects of rationalism and scientific materialism had influenced both Catholic and Protestant theologians. But, nevertheless, the ordinary people in both streams still maintained their strong belief in the supernatural, as they do to this day.

Nevertheless, because most Catholic and Protestant leaders have not picked up on the centrality of healing and its need to accompany the preaching of the Gospel, people who are desperate and who cannot find help in their churches sometimes go looking elsewhere. All over the world, on every continent, Christians have turned to the native healer: the "curandero," the shaman, the witch doctor. When my wife, Judith, who grew up in the hills of Kentucky, was sick as a little girl, her mother took her to visit a "traditional healer" to seek her healing.

But something else is happening on a worldwide scale: Pentecostal Christians have, in the last hundred years, rediscovered the power of the Holy Spirit, together with the willingness of God to heal and free

His people. They do not see healing as something rare and reserved to a special class of people. They are returning to the model of the early Church, the deepest tradition: "Everybody gets to play." These Pentecostal-evangelical-charismatic churches are growing at an explosive rate.

The more classical Protestants—Anglicans, Presbyterians, Methodists—are no longer growing (except for those who have become charismatic). And Roman Catholics in some countries are feeling threatened by the decline in their enrollments as people flock to these growing churches where they see the power of God at work. Countries like Guatemala, which a few years ago were 95 percent Catholic, are now perhaps 40 percent Protestant—evangelical or Pentecostal. One Catholic response has been to label them as "sects," and come up with all kinds of reasons why their people have left, some of which are partly true ("American Protestants have come in here with all kinds of financial aid"). But I don't think that response even begins to touch the reality of what is happening.

The mainline churches have had a vacuum at the heart of the Gospel's presentation. The people have been seeking God's help—the "Kingdom of God"—in healing and deliverance, but for centuries leaders have not fully provided it. Where, for example, do we find seminaries—Protestant and Catholic—providing full-length courses in healing prayer and deliverance from evil spirits? Fifty years ago, loyalty to one's denomination was often fierce, but now those ties are loosening. Large numbers of Christians—Catholic and Protestant—are seeking services where they find vibrant life and are changing church affiliation to be a part of it.

These Pentecostal Christians have stepped into the gap. The largest church in the world is in Seoul, Korea, and the second largest is in Santiago, Chile. And they are both Pentecostal.

The established churches should, instead of criticizing these Pentecostal churches, see in them a positive model of what needs to be done and what people all over the world have been seeking. They are seeking God and His power to help them become a new creation.

And when they find Him, they will rip a hole in the roof to be let down into His presence.[17]

20

FIRES START
(AND ARE PUT OUT)

W e have now seen the broad picture of divine healing stretched
out over two thousand years of history.

First came the first three centuries of Christianity during which
healing prayer remained as a major part of normal, ordinary life. Then,
during the following sixteen centuries, healing was progressively weakened and pushed off to the side. Paradoxically, the decline of healing
began by honoring miraculous healing and putting it so high on a
pedestal that no ordinary person would presume to pray for healing.
Ministers of healing were almost idolized so that only extraordinary
saints were regarded as capable of healing. By the year 500 the only
ones you were sure were this holy were the saints in heaven, no longer
walking this earth, and healing was relegated to making pilgrimages
to shrines and praying for the intercession of these saints.

Another thousand years down the road the Protestant reformers,
ironically, proved to be even more devastating to the Christian healing ministry. Here the strongest voice was John Calvin's. He strongly
affirmed his belief in the remarkable healings worked by Jesus and
His apostles when they laid their hands upon the sick. But Calvin also

claimed that the healing ministry ceased after they had died; and, for him, the only thing left after the first century was superstition.

Several centuries later, in the eighteenth century, some theologians went still further and denied that supernatural healing and exorcism had ever taken place, even in Jesus' life—that it was all a "myth"—which had deep spiritual meaning but no literal reality.

But so central was healing to the Gospel story that any intelligent person, reading the New Testament, would at least have to ask the question, "Where did it all go?" From time to time, some questing Christians—usually ministers—would be propelled by desperate circumstances into praying for the sick. To their surprise, these adventurous pastors would find that prayer actually worked to heal. Then the ordinary people, who never seem to lose their hope in healing prayer whenever they find a leader willing to try it, would proceed to make this healer famous.

But the amazing thing is that when these inquirers try it out and find that Jesus still heals today, the news is not given a joyous reception; the facts are met with skepticism, if not downright opposition. In fact, when someone makes this hopeful discovery and has the courage to act on it, we discover a regular pattern.

1. The curious individuals who ask the bold question are usually devoted to reading and trying to understand the meaning of Scripture.
2. Then they back away; they are reluctant to pray for the sick because it goes counter to everything they have learned. They are afraid to be seen as fanatics by their superiors or fellow Christians. This reluctance is even stronger when it comes to casting out evil spirits.
3. Then they meet a desperate situation where prayer is the only possible solution (for example, in desperation Martin Luther prayed for his sick friend Melanchthon).
4. Then they see an astonishing healing. Thus encouraged, they pray to heal the sick again—and again.
5. Next come the crowds. Desperate people show up seeking help. Publicity follows and the authorities hear about it.
6. Following great success comes the opposition—usually from within the Church.

7. This opposition takes steps to close down the upstart healing ministry. If that doesn't work, the entrenched leadership works to shut off the healing ministry and confine it to a small area where it cannot touch most people. A successful healing ministry is treated like an infection that needs to be encapsulated (just as the human body walls off an infection, forming it into a boil so it cannot invade the rest of the body).

Let's take time, in this chapter to look at individuals with fascinating stories who—in the face of such opposition—were willing to explore the possibility of healing.

Johann Christophe Blumhardt

We begin with one particularly fascinating and instructive case, the story of Johann Christophe Blumhardt (1805–1880), an obscure Lutheran pastor from the Black Forest area of Germany.[1] (He was obscure, that is, until he personally became involved in the deliverance/healing ministry in 1841.) He had been appointed as curate of Möttlingen, a little town numbering 535 people. His parish was spiritually lethargic and his congregation regularly slept through his dutifully prepared sermons. (He loved the Bible and had read through it twice by the time he was twelve.)

Then he was reluctantly drawn into a struggle that he tried to avoid. Blumhardt was a friendly, moderate pastor, the least likely kind of person to get involved in controversy, but he had a problem parishioner. Göttlieben Dittus was a misshapen woman with a disagreeable temperament whom everyone in the village walked across the street to avoid. She suffered from various mysterious diseases, notably, a strange bleeding that oozed from her breasts.

Her physician came to the conclusion (surprising for that era) that her many ailments were spiritual in origin and that he could not help her. For one thing, she would fall to the floor unconscious whenever grace was said. Naturally, her family (two brothers and two sisters) came to their pastor, Blumhardt, for help. This problem could not be kept secret, because strange sounds were heard coming from her house, and this roused the curiosity of the villagers.

With great reluctance Blumhardt decided that it was his ecclesiastical duty to investigate the situation. As a conservative Christian, he was afraid this case might involve spiritualism, since he knew that many witches in the Black Forest practiced magic and spells. Eventually, he decided to visit Göttlieben, whose response was to drop at his feet, unconscious, in a heap.

None of this had been covered in his seminary course in Tübingen, and so, wondering what to do, he studied his Bible, seeking guidance. When he next came to visit her, a big crowd had gathered, attracted by the loud noises coming from her home. Being naturally cautious, Blumhardt decided he could not do any harm by asking her to repeat after him, "Lord Jesus, help me." When she did this, to their astonishment, the breast bleeding ceased.

Over the course of the next two years, when he prayed for her in simple ways, hundreds of demons seemed to leave her. The process was often difficult and violent; she would go into convulsions and, at times, she would even physically attack people. At one point the spirits within her yelled out, "We are 1,067!" If nothing else, Blumhardt was patient and determined, a good German pastor, obedient to what he saw as the demands of the Gospel.

Finally, in the Christmas season of 1843, there was one last violent spiritual battle, during which Blumhardt prayed to free Göttlieben in a session lasting from two A.M. until dawn. One extraordinary result was that her numerous physical ailments were also healed (a short leg, an elevated shoulder and stomach problems). After this her whole disposition changed—so much so that Blumhardt's wife entrusted the care of their four children to Göttlieben, and she became a close family friend.

The still more amazing result was that Blumhardt's sleepy church and the entire village underwent a spiritual "awakening." Villagers would unexpectedly start to weep and spontaneously repent of their sins. This repentance also touched hundreds from the surrounding villages—and was accompanied not only by weeping but by profound life changes. Again, spontaneously, without his encouraging it, penitents came to Blumhardt and confessed their sins. He learned to lay his hands on them and assure them that God had forgiven them—although this also was not part of what he had learned in the seminary. Eventually, people lined up to see him, beginning every day at 6:30

in the morning, and he would see them, one at a time, until 11:30 at night. On one day he met with 35 persons individually, and as word spread throughout the region, someone counted visitors from 176 surrounding villages who came to his church one Sunday morning!

And yet Blumhardt remained a humble man who refused to use high-pressure tactics to convert people. He did not even hold healing services. He was worried about seeming to steal parishioners from other churches. Strife never flourished around him and he refused to divide people into groups of the "converted" and "unconverted," the "saved" and the "lost." Finally, through his gentle approach, the entire village was converted. He trusted in the basic goodness of the people, and no one ever felt ignored.

Accompanying this God-initiated repentance were many healings, although Blumhardt refused to publicize them. And yet they were remarkable. To prevent the people from going to folk-healers and spiritualists, he dared occasionally to lay his hands on the sick and many were healed—physically, spiritually and emotionally. Even cattle were healed and Blumhardt's fame kept growing.

With such remarkable, beneficial results, coming from such a self-effacing man who was quietly respectful of authority, you would think he might meet universal approbation from the authorities, both Church and state (which at that time were joined). But, as in our pattern given above, the more wonderful the healings, the more the opposition grew.

Most of the neighboring pastors, for example, distanced themselves from Blumhardt, even though they liked him. They whispered about "Blumhardt's special theory." He was accused of acting like a Catholic priest by hearing confessions, although he stoutly affirmed that he was Lutheran, not Catholic! He defended his telling people that their sins were forgiven because their lives were transformed: "By their fruits you will know them."

Then he started getting attacked from another side: the medical profession. Physicians complained that he was infringing on their rights: Sick people should come only to doctors to be healed. His own church's consistory concurred, commanding him to tell the people that they should not expect to receive help from God directly. In short, "If you're sick, see a doctor." And yet, Blumhardt had always told the sick to see their doctors. His fellow pastors approached the medical question by telling him that a pastor's job was to tell the sick that they were meant to endure their sufferings courageously. He should console them by telling them how much blessing their sicknesses brought them.

Finally, the authorities forbade him to include healing as part of his mission. His response was, "I shall no longer lay hands on any stranger. But I will still listen to them. If miracles continue, don't blame me." Later (1846) he bowed even more to criticism and refused to see visitors in private.

He tried to obey the authorities and agreed not to lay hands on any stranger.[2] "Come to church, listen to the sermon and lay your suffering before the Savior." The stream of visitors started falling off considerably. In spite of all this, Blumhardt was officially reprimanded.[3]

You would think that Blumhardt was the ideal kind of person to restore the healing ministry to Germany. He was the opposite of the stereotype of a "faith healer." He was repulsed by attempts to publicize healing testimonies. People in the little town loved him like a father and he had a model family of four children. Visitors remarked on how loving the entire town had become and how strife had disappeared. His style of prayer was unemotional and unbelievably simple: "Jesus, please help."

And yet the opposition grew.

At last he decided to leave Möttlingen; his friends got together and bought an unprofitable spa, Bäd Boll, where he moved with his family in 1852. There he was finally left in peace by the authorities. Restrictions were lifted and sometimes a hundred and fifty visitors would stay at the spa. Once more healing started happening. Blumhardt seldom made enemies and his staff could be seen there, sitting in the courtyard and discussing questions with him, cigar in hand. Everyone liked him and he acted in a most moderate manner. And yet, he could not put a dent in the establishment's ban on healing.

He summed up his life's struggle with statements such as, "The first thing that is needed is the conversion of Christendom. . . . Only a fraction of the promise was fulfilled at the time of the apostles. Must it not now be fulfilled on a larger scale? This stream of the Spirit will come—let us await it in confidence. The thirst is almost killing us, and people are deteriorating both inwardly and outwardly."[4]

Other Christians Who Rediscovered Healing

Just as Blumhardt, a Lutheran, rediscovered God's willingness to heal, so we find that the same thing happened to other seeking Christians who came from a wide variety of denominations: Puritan, Episcopal, Baptist and Presbyterian. They all had an extraordinary success at first, but then they were eventually smothered by opposition—not from outside so much as from the inside of their own churches.

The recurring pattern is really extraordinary. Let's just take a look at the United States during the eighteenth and nineteenth centuries.

Jonathan Edwards

Perhaps the most famous Puritan preacher and theologian in early American history was Jonathan Edwards. His powerful sermons occasioned a famous revival in Northampton, Massachusetts, in 1734, a precursor of the Great Awakening that was soon to come. What is not so well known is that this revival lasted only about two years and the opposition to Edwards's ministry came from theologians in his own denomination. The main criticism to Edwards centered on what today would be regarded as common manifestations of the Holy Spirit's power. Two things, in particular, stirred up controversy.

One criticism centered on Abigail Hutchison, a dying woman who came to one of Edwards's meetings. There she experienced an overwhelming sense of God's glory, an experience so strong that her physical strength failed and she had to be lain on a bed. In charismatic circles today, this fainting phenomenon happens frequently and is called "resting in the Spirit" or "being slain in the Spirit." Later, in the Great Awakening, in John Wesley's and George Whitefield's meetings, this fainting experience became common. But in Edwards's day it was regarded as a sign of overemotionalism demonstrating that his ministry was unbalanced.

The second criticism was caused when a layman from the nearby village of South Hadley made the audacious claim that laymen were capable of ministering to others! This man actually had the nerve to pray for a person who was suffering from depression. This was seen as encroaching on a duty reserved only for clergy. Moreover, this same man proclaimed that one day there would be a revival in which the gifts of the Spirit would be released again as in the Acts of the Apostles.

Today, of course, these beliefs have become commonplace, but in 1735 they were seen as heretical. Edwards himself told this man that he was in error. Shortly afterward, Edwards admitted that the Holy Spirit seemed to have withdrawn from his meetings. From 1736 to 1740 Edwards tried to rekindle the revival, but it had died out. Perhaps Edwards himself, in his timidity, had helped stifle it.

In Boston, Edwards had many critics, so he defended the revival in a commencement sermon at Yale (1741), in which he freely admitted that the revival in Northampton showed some excesses. But he tried to persuade the traditionalists that great value lay in what was happening. Here, in Edwards, we have a Puritan—a Calvinist—who rediscovered some of the gifts of the Spirit, but who was shut down by opposition and also impeded by some of his own fears.[5] Edwards went on to receive acclaim for his theological writings on topics such as the relation between free will and predestination, but the revival activity in his parish only went on for two short periods, totaling about five years.

George Whitefield and the Great Awakening

In 1739, George Whitefield, the famous preacher and colleague of John and Charles Wesley, whose preaching was stirring revival, came to the American colonies to preach. Whitefield was an Anglican and did not realize at that time that Anglicanism could not absorb the "overemotional" manifestations that accompanied their preaching and that eventually led to the founding of the Methodist Church. (John Wesley died believing that he was a good Anglican).

Whitefield was extraordinarily successful. He managed to preach in 40 cities and towns in 45 days to thousands of people at a time, traveling all the way from Maine to South Carolina. Even Ben Franklin was astounded at the power of Whitefield's preaching and how thousands could hear him (without a microphone, of course) and understand him—and be converted on Boston Common.

Whitefield also managed to squeeze in three days of preaching in Edwards's church and, again, there followed some remarkable physical manifestations—people crying out, fainting, singing and praying for hours. Some people rested in the Spirit for up to 24 hours at a time and others experienced visions of heaven.

This Great Awakening had a profound effect in the Colonies and led to a great increase of members in the Methodist and Baptist churches, while those who resisted—the Anglicans and Presbyterians—declined in influence. Before Whitefield came to the Colonies, the Anglicans and Presbyterians had the largest churches. Afterward, the Methodists and Baptists predominated. (A major reason for the shift in membership numbers was that the Anglicans and Presbyterians required seminary training for their ministers; on the frontier, the Methodists and Baptists had simpler requirements.)

But again there was resistance. Part of the opposition arose because of excesses by a few revival leaders after Whitefield had left the Colonies and returned to England. In particular, these preachers became highly critical of the established churches and concentrated their attacks on the clergy. One Gilbert Tennent, for example, suggested that self-appointed laymen should inquire into the spiritual state of their pastors and even encouraged some congregations to depose their unenlightened pastors. He even claimed that several pastors were unconverted hypocrites. Another revivalist, James Davenport, believed he had a special ability to discern the spiritual state of clergymen. He went from town to town, summoning the clergy to appear before him for judgment. Couple this with some of the emotional excesses that occurred in revival meetings and you can see why opposition grew within the churches.

Edwards wrote extensively and persuasively, trying to defend the value of these revivals by weighing the enormous good that resulted against the excesses of imprudent, independent preachers who refused to recognize their arrogance and the harm they were doing. He had to defend the Great Awakening from the attacks of traditional, overly rational theologians who fought to keep things the way they were.

One of these was a highly respected theologian named Charles Chauncey, who pastored Boston's most prestigious church, the First Church of Boston (Congregational) from 1727 until he died in 1787.[6] The church was named "Old Brick" and that became Chauncey's nickname, too. "Old Brick" was an excellent scholar and a disciplined individual. At noon, for example, he took exactly one pinch of snuff—his only sniff for that day.

He equated the Great Awakening with irrationality and emotionalism (which they termed "Enthusiasm"). The swooning, visions and other "mystical" phenomena, he connected with the hated Catholicism. He was especially critical of extemporaneous preaching, which he believed was simply an excuse for preachers who were too lazy to do scriptural research and write out their sermons. (Many lay preachers had sprung up in the revival who had not been to seminary but believed that God had given them a call to preach.) The final blow, driving Chauncey over the edge, happened when James Davenport, the self-appointed discerner, appeared at Chauncey's home uninvited and commanded Chauncey to give an account of his soul. Chauncey's response was to give Davenport a tongue-lashing and show him the door.

Chauncey then moved into action and tried to refute Edwards point by point by writing a book called *Seasonable Thoughts on the State of Religion in New England*, a caricature detailing all the abuses that Chauncey could gather together in one volume. This book became an instant and huge bestseller, and this crushed Edwards's influence. Both Harvard and Yale, the main seminaries of that day, passed resolutions condemning "Enthusiasm" and the Great Awakening.

When Whitefield returned to the Colonies in 1744, he found that most pulpits were now closed to him. The Awakening was over (until another wave came following the Revolution).

Like Gamaliel, Jonathan Edwards warned the authorities that they had better not turn their backs on what God was doing in the Awakening, nor oppose it. He even threatened that the curse of God might fall on those who opposed this move of God. But he lost out and was asked to resign his pastorate in Northampton. He moved to a smaller church in Stockbridge, Massachusetts, where he had plenty of free time to write his famous theological tracts. He recovered his scholarly fame, and shortly before he died he was offered the presidency of Princeton, but he never again took a personal part in revivals once he had left his church in Northampton.

Here we see that same pattern: The Holy Spirit moves but is blocked in the institutional churches. Part of the reason is doctrinal—the same old arguments we have seen earlier in this book—and part is because of excesses and aberrations that give the renewal a bad name. Usually, the institutional churches resist what seems new (although the renewal impulse is as old as the book of Acts). Those who side with renewal often end up having to start one more independent body (for example, the Methodists or the Vineyard), if they wish to remain faithful to their vision.

How ironic that what we generally regard as the greatest movements in American Church history were stopped in their tracks shortly after they began! The Great Awakening, for instance, is a famous event and people who know even a little about American religious history know that George Whitefield once preached to twenty thousand people in Boston Common and that Ben Franklin, the deist, was mightily impressed. (Deism is the belief that God exists but is uninvolved in the world.) And yet, when Whitefield returned from England just a few years later, most pulpits were closed to him. All this reminds us of how Jesus once said that His contemporaries honored the prophets of old and adorned their tombs, but stoned the living prophets that walked their streets.

The healing (and deliverance) ministry is so clearly a part of the Gospel that inquisitive Christians, no matter what denomination they belong to, inevitably are led to ask, Whatever happened to healing? Why did it disappear? This, of course, is the question we are here addressing. We have seen what happened to Johann Christophe Blumhardt, although he seemed to possess the ideal, balanced temperament that would lead to his modest, unobtrusive healing ministry being accepted. A century earlier, in the American colonies, the astonishing manifestations of the Spirit's power that accompanied the preaching of Jonathan Edwards and George Whitefield were accepted by the people but were walled off by the clergy. Instead of building their tombs, we erect their statues, but ignore the prophetic lessons they teach while they are alive.

But these were not the only ones to reawaken the healing ministry. It is fascinating to see how, at the end of the nineteenth century, inquiring Christian leaders from several denominations stepped forward and started praying for the sick, and then opposition developed from their officials. Unfortunately, these pastors were not all as balanced as Blumhardt, and they gave their opponents real cause for criticism.

Here are several brief biographies of a few of these pioneers who came from a variety of religious backgrounds. These are just a few among many, but these particular innovators all lived in the small area of Boston, Massachusetts.

Episcopalians

Dr. Charles Cullis,[7] a Boston physician, was working with tuberculosis patients when he began wrestling with the famous healing passage in James 5:14–16. He finally started praying with his patients and soon witnessed several major healing miracles. This led to his combining the medical treatment of his patients with prayer for their healing. The press praised his work, but the clergy, influenced by Calvin's Cessationism, criticized him. As an Episcopalian he believed that faith and medicine could work together, and he cited Ecclesiasticus 38[8] to support his work.

Being a doctor, rather than a clergyman, he was free to set up a healing home in Beacon Hill, Massachusetts, where he held healing services. Still more important, he taught healing prayer to thousands of people. The "Faith-Cure" movement, which he started, turned out to be the first sustained healing movement of modern Christendom. His teaching was balanced, but his life was somewhat out of balance in that he died of overwork at the age of 59 (1892). Unfortunately, his healing home did not last, but his teaching influenced others who then carried on the healing ministry—leaders and authors such as A. J. Gordon, A. B. Simpson and Carrie Judd Montgomery.[9]

Carrie Judd Montgomery was also an Episcopalian who lived a long life (1858–1946) and helped found the Christian & Missionary Alliance, an important non-Cessationist denomination. When she was young she injured her back so severely that she was kept homebound as a complete invalid. Since healing was not then part of the Episcopal Church's practice, she reached out to an African-American healer, who wrote and told her that she would pray for her "in faith" at a certain hour. She instructed Carrie to pray for herself and then act, by getting out of bed and walking, no matter how she felt. Carrie did this and was healed although, before this, she had not even been able to get out of bed.

She wrote an influential book, *The Prayer of Faith*, based on her own experience. Her view was that the highest expression of faith resulted when the physical evidence of sickness contradicted a Bible promise. Then you were to walk in faith and disregard the evidence of your senses. She was careful to state (as others later did not) that invalids are not to claim that they *feel* better unless they really do, but they can state that they *are* being made whole, on the authority of God's word.

Her own experience led her to believe that taking medicine or seeing a physician would be a sign of weak faith, although she did not totally condemn seeking a physician's help. You don't hear much about her today, but she had a profound effect on the faith-healing movement, both because of her popular book and also because she lived well into her eighties and, with her wealthy husband's support, was able to travel widely and speak about her beliefs.

We should learn from the fact that she started out in the Episcopal Church but soon moved into other Christian circles, as do so many today when their spiritual hunger is not satisfied. Like so many others, whose advice helps some but not everyone, she magnified her individual, personal experience of faith and made it into a general teaching. Her particular theological grid was this: Rather than see medicine and faith working together, and God using both, she considered medicine a second-rate healing channel for those with imperfect faith. And yet she led many followers to a belief in Christ's desire to heal.

You notice that some of these healing pioneers were laypeople who were not constricted by their churches' authority and teaching. In some ways this was an advantage, but it meant that those who were extreme in their views did not have a counterbalance of colleagues with some sense of history and understanding of Scripture.

Baptists

And now we come to a Baptist pastor, A. J. Gordon (1836–1895),[10] who got involved in the healing ministry through Dr. Cullis. Gordon was a very successful pastor and preacher—again, in Boston—and his influence still remains in Gordon College, a mission institute he founded and which was named for him.

When he discovered that healing prayer worked, he had to sort through all the Dispensationalism and Cessationist arguments that assailed him. He worked it all out to his satisfaction, like Darby, by claiming that we are now living in a new era, a new dispensation of Church history. In accord with his Baptist tradition, he was strongly anti-Catholic; so he considered that all the Catholic stories of healing miracles after the time of Constantine were simply satanic fraud. He read widely (for instance, he admired Johann Christophe Blumhardt), but he consulted only Protestant sources.

In time, he wrote an influential, well thought-out book on Christian healing, *The Ministry of Healing: Miracles of Cure in All Ages*, which is still in circulation. Gordon defended healing on two fronts: He fought first against the Cessationists who taught that miracles had ceased, and he also criticized Mary Baker Eddy and Christian Science as being neither truly Christian nor scientific.

With prophetic insight Gordon argued that if the healing revival was ignored, the liberal theologians would continue to gain ascendancy and evangelical Christianity would be placed in severe jeopardy. Gordon understood that the long-standing separation between the Bible and experience brought on by radical cessationism was on the verge of overwhelming the mainline denominations as it had in the old Congregationalist church (the Puritans) which produced unitarianism.

Although Gordon was largely successful in his Boston pastorate, he did not convert the majority of Baptists to his belief in healing, as we may readily observe today, a hundred and fifty years later.[11]

Anti-Medical Zealots[12]

Unfortunately, after Dr. Cullis, the leaders in the healing ministry gradually moved in the direction of teaching that true believers should turn aside from medicine. Following the controversy on evolution, science and religion continued to move toward confrontation, not cooperation. A Methodist, Ethan O. Allen, taught that you had to make a choice between faith and medication. A. B. Simpson, a Presbyterian, wrote an influential book—still in print—which declared that medicine is man's way but the true Christian should repudiate it in favor of God's way: faith.

The most extreme of all, John Alexander Dowie (1847–1907), came from a Scotch Pentecostal background, and was a powerful, sarcastic speaker who founded two hundred local congregations, together with an entire community, Zion City, on the outskirts of Chicago, Illinois. A brilliant debater and very authoritarian, he incurred the opposition of pastors, politicians and the medical establishment by proclaiming that medicine was merely licensed quackery. Missionaries in Africa and Asia who accepted his teachings died of malaria because they refused to take medication. After Dowie's death, his movement fell apart, but the anti-medical bias of the Christian healing movement remains. In reaction, the medical profession largely came to view "faith-healers" as practicing "unlicensed quackery."

Here again we see individual Christians—Episcopalians, Baptists, Presbyterians and Methodists—reading Scripture and enthusiastically rediscovering the healing ministry. Some of them were successful for a time, but for the most part, the established churches were not touched. For some, their work died with them, while others attracted criticism because of their unbalanced views.

The Attackers[13]

At the end of the nineteenth century, the largest Protestant denomination in the United States was the Methodist Church. The Methodist establishment was effectively steered away from healing, exorcism and the gifts of the Spirit by James Buckley (1836–1920). In the influential *Christian Advocate* (he was editor), he gave out a natural explanation for healing and deliverance. Healing was simply psychosomatic, and he judged that Christians who prayed for healing were doing the very same thing as Christian Scientists. He even compared faith healing to astrology. He was a convinced Cessationist and through a string of editorials written over many years, he managed to marginalize the Faith-Cure Movement. By the 1890s the movement withered up and was refused a hearing by the Protestant establishment.

> He played a key role in turning the Methodist denomination away from healing and Pentecostalism at a time when Methodism was a hair's breath away from being the first mainline denomination to embrace both. . . .

What the history of American Christianity would have been like if Methodism had become a Pentecostal denomination in the 1890's can only be imagined.[14]

This turn of events is ironic, considering that, one hundred and fifty years earlier, the Methodist founders Wesley and Whitefield were criticized for the unusual religious outpourings that they experienced in their meetings: healings, exorcisms, "swoonings" and loud weeping.

When many of these same manifestations touched people in the early days of the Pentecostal revivals on the frontier and later at Azusa Street, the now well-established Methodist Church wrote them off and forced them into founding still more new churches (such as the Assemblies of God), instead of welcoming all these manifestations as possible signs of new life and a pouring out of the Spirit.

A leader in shutting down the Presbyterians and Calvinists was the eminent teacher and author Benjamin Warfield (1851–1921), who won the field and kept the reborn ministry of healing out of the Calvinist churches.[15] Warfield exercised tremendous influence because he taught 2,700 students at Princeton and was editor of the prestigious *Princeton Theological Review*, which was regarded by evangelicals as the last word in orthodoxy. Warfield wrote a powerful book, *Counterfeit Miracles*, whose title shows his Cessationist point of view and is still quoted today by evangelicals.

Warfield taught that miracles ceased with the death of the last apostle and that, once the Church had been established, demons had been banished and could no longer harm Christians. He taught that Catholic belief in miracles—including the teaching of St. Augustine—represented a return to paganism. He discounted Pentecostalism as simple emotionalism. He devoted an entire chapter to criticizing the healing homes of Dr. Cullis and discounted the healings that happened in these homes as simply due to the power of suggestion.

By the time Warfield and Buckley finished their long teaching and writing careers, healing was seen by most Protestants as, at best, an illusion, or at worst, heresy. The Pentecostal groups and churches were written off as cults. (We can see why the Pentecostals have, in turn, written off the World Council of Churches—whose members include the Presbyterians and Methodists, the spiritual descendants of Warfield and Buckley—as demonically inspired organizations.)

As a result, healing, a major theme of the gospels, has remained largely unexamined by Protestant theologians. Typical Protestant historians have also ignored Pentecostal history. A combination of influences—Cessationism, Dispensationalism and demythologizing—has joined to shut out healing from most churches today. The Reverend Morton Kelsey, writing in 1973, said that in his experience he found medical doctors to be far more open to healing prayer than were ministers and pastors. Kelsey stated that

> There is no theology which is accepted or approved by any major modern church which has a place for the direct action of God in any of the gifts of the Spirit, healing included.[16]

As we will see in our exploration of the explosion of Holy Spirit power in the twentieth century, the path was being cleared for various parts of the Church to experience the charismata. Even so, Kelsey's comment shows that most churches in the traditional denominations were still skeptical about the gifts.

However we may understand the reasons[17] for this opposition to such gifts of the Spirit as healing and prophecy, the pattern is fascinating to trace out. Once we see the pattern we should be better able to avoid the mistakes of the past.

John Gardner, founder of Common Cause, the influential citizen's lobby, wrote a marvelously insightful book, *Self-Renewal*,[18] in which he talks about how every institution tends, after twenty years, to ossify and to fight against change. To counter this deadening process, he states that every aging institution desperately needs prophets who can point out what needs changing. Unfortunately, the institution usually tries to silence anyone who suggests change. This prophet is labeled as disruptive and disloyal. The health of every aging institution depends on its ability to protect the dissenter in case he or she turns out to be the prophet who is needed for the growth—or even the survival—of the institution.

Unfortunately, the first restraining force for one who steps off the paths of custom and majority opinion is not the lethal gunfire of opponents but the clutching hands of intimates and colleagues.[19]

Some of the individuals who rediscovered the power of prayer for healing were not as balanced as Cullis and Blumhardt (the latter, as we have seen, was exiled to a spa, anyway). The unbalanced teachers brought the term *faith-healer* into disrepute at a time when we desperately need to restore an authentic healing ministry. And yet we do not even have a positive term for someone who prays for healing. (Was Jesus a "faith-healer"?)

In the past hundred years, however, numbers of Christians have rediscovered divine healing and have multiplied to such an extent that the healing ministry—while it has not entered the field of study of most theologians—must be acknowledged. The Pentecostal churches are exploding in number and influence all around the world, while the charismatic renewal within the established churches has grown in credibility and influence. To take just one example, in November 2001, the Vatican invited 99 persons from all over the world to take part in an international colloquium on healing (there it was reported that the International Association of Exorcists has grown from a membership of seven priests in 1993 to hundreds ten years later).[20]

The main danger, as I see it, is that the healing ministry has now met with approval to a limited degree, but there is a glass ceiling that tends to limit healing to a "certain group of enthusiasts who appreciate that kind of spirituality." And yet the Church has a huge need to understand the power of prayer to solve its deepest problems and needs—both as an institution and as a community of individual, wounded Christians.

Just to take one example, approximately 25 million women in the United States have been victims of sexual abuse. This kind of abuse usually leaves permanent psychological and spiritual damage. At the time of this writing, 145 male victims of priests' sexual abuse in the United States have committed suicide.[21] And yet, to my knowledge, no authority in the Catholic Church has proposed that prayer for inner healing might help or even cure the sense of shame that led these young men to take their lives. (And this is just one example out of many.) Most leaders are aware that counseling can help, but they still seem unaware—or are perhaps skeptical—of the extraordinary benefits of healing prayer. We have discovered, in fact, that through prayer the damage can be healed.

We have not even begun to explore the depths of healing that can take place when we pray. And people's lives depend on it!

21

PENTECOST RETURNS

The Twentieth Century

W hen we take a look at the fires of renewal that sprang up in the eighteenth and nineteenth centuries through various individuals, we cannot help but notice that they did not involve a total renewal and rediscovery of the Holy Spirit's power and charisms. They were marked by a recovery of this-or-that gift but, ordinarily, not of the baptism in the Spirit accompanied by all the charisms. All these revivals were powerful but partial.

Still, the rediscovery of healing touched pastors and leaders in all the denominations—the Anglicans (the Wesleyan revival, which eventually became the Methodist Church), the Calvinists (Jonathan Edwards and the Awakening in Northampton, Massachusetts), the Presbyterians (J. Cameron Peddie in Scotland), the Baptists (A. J. Gordon in Boston), the Lutherans (Johann Christophe Blumhardt in Germany), and Episcopalians (Dr. Charles Cullis, also in Boston), and so on. In every denomination, in every place, God seemed to touch individuals with a healing gift.

It was as if God was trying to start a fire, wherever He found a hearth, dry wood and someone with a match. But then someone else would notice the smoke, get worried, call the fire department and put out the fire. Ironically, the best-known, long-lasting healing ministry of the nineteenth century was established by the Christian Scientists, who were regarded by most Christians as unorthodox.

In America, although many individual small charismatic fires were put out, increasingly significant outbreaks all through the eighteenth and nineteenth centuries—the Wesley-Whitefield revival and Great Awakening; the Second Great Awakening ignited by Finney's preaching—were credited with saving much of American Protestantism from becoming deist. These revivals were accompanied by many dramatic manifestations of the Spirit, such as the "falling" phenomenon (later called "being slain in the Spirit" and, later still, as "resting in the Spirit"). Some of these revivals resulted in new churches being formed, such as the Fire Baptized Holiness Church, whose very name stimulates our imaginations to think of the dramatic manifestations that accompanied the revivals on the American frontier.

Cane Ridge, Kentucky

One of the more influential—and fascinating—revivals during these years was the great camp meeting that took place on the first day of a new century, January 1, 1800, in Cane Ridge, Kentucky, sixty miles west of Lexington. In those days, Kentucky had only recently been opened to settlement by Daniel Boone.

The spiritual situation on the frontier (although a number of lesser revivals also broke out in Kentucky about the same time) was dismal. The population was composed of settlers who had hewn out little clearings in the wilderness and were famous, not for their holiness, but for violence and the powerful moonshine they manufactured in their primitive stills. Pastors described the frontier as being filled with vice—rampant drunkenness, avaricious land grabbing accompanied by murder.

One Methodist, James Smith, who was visiting Kentucky a few years before Cane Ridge (1795), was worried about the religious condition of the people whose meager beliefs were moving in the direction of deism. The newly founded Methodist Church, the most popular in those days, had already gone down in numbers nationally from 67,643 to 61,351.[1]

The response of Presbyterian and Methodist preachers was to fast and pray, and they collaborated—a very unusual phenomenon—in preaching several revivals. When several Presbyterian pastors announced that they would hold a Communion service in Cane Ridge, to everyone's amazement, an estimated 25,000 people came flocking to the meeting, an astonishing number considering the sparsely populated forests. They arrived on horseback and in wagons and camped in the open; some men slept under their wagons, while the women rested inside. Others crowded into cabins. It was a tremendous feeling of expectancy that drew people from all over the frontier.

Part of the people's motivation was, undoubtedly, that these lonely pioneer families, isolated in the forests, wanted to meet up with their fellow settlers. A few even came to scoff at the religious part of the meeting, but the fiery preaching soon took effect and many of the frontier people lingered on and spent nearly a week, praying and listening to sermons.

The most amazing thing was what happened to the people. Multitudes were overcome with remorse and wept for their sins, experiencing conversions that lasted. And also present were all the extraordinary phenomena that they believed signaled a new Pentecost. People were falling and shouting. Some of the preachers claimed that, while they spoke, they were in an ecstasy. People claimed that they experienced the manifest presence of God.

Estimates of the slain in the Spirit ranged from one thousand to three thousand; those who took Communion, from eight hundred to three thousand; and those who were converted, from one thousand to three thousand.[2] One observer described "sinners dropping down on every hand, shrieking, groaning, crying for mercy, convoluted . . . agonizing, fainting, falling down in distress for sinners, or in raptures of joy!"[3]

Although there were emotional excesses, the Cane Ridge revival (and others like it in such obscure locations as Muddy River, Claylick and Little Muddy Creek), created an altogether different spiritual climate on the frontier. Visitors who came a year after declared that the frontier had been spiritually transformed. Using the criterion, "By their fruits you shall know them," these wild revivals seem to have been genuinely of God.

Ask most people in the United States if they have ever heard of Cane Ridge and they will probably answer no. Remember that Thomas Jefferson had predicted that the common religion of the United States would soon become Universalism.[4] Jefferson's prophecy did not come true and part of the reason was that Cane Ridge had a profound effect upon religion that has lasted to this day. It was one of those influences that enabled the United States to remain a largely Christian nation.[5]

Although these camp meetings and other dramatic spiritual events were compared to the original Pentecost, nevertheless, some of the most important charismatic gifts, such as healing, did not seem to be a major part of these revivals—nor was praying in tongues. The major revival of healing, along with the baptism in the Holy Spirit, had to wait until the next century, the twentieth.

Enter the Twentieth Century

As we have said, certain individual Christians rediscovered the healing ministry in the eighteenth and nineteenth centuries—in almost every denomination. But the little fires that they started were soon contained and they failed to touch the majority of Christians who never even knew that these Christian healers existed.

Nevertheless, the Wesleyans and the camp revivalists of those same two centuries directed remarkable preaching events that led to massive repentance. These movements truly changed lives and, in addition, were publicized by extraordinary spiritual, emotional and physical manifestations—such as visions, "fallings," and "signs and wonders"—calling to mind that first Pentecost.

Again, it was the same old pattern, God choosing the uneducated, marginalized people in out of the way places. ("Can anything good come out of Nazareth"—or out of Cane Ridge—or Muddy Creek?) What had not been revealed to the wise and learned was being revealed to the simple and the poor. In consequence, these astonishing events barely attracted the attention of those in the establishment, such as the Congregationalists and the Episcopalians, and could be dismissed as overemotional, hysterical outbursts of ignorant people, "hillbillies."

And it was true: Most of the Methodist preachers had never gone to seminary. The early American Methodists asked four questions about any candidate for the ministry, the first being, "Is this man truly converted?" and the fourth being, "Has he a horse?" Such were the heroic demands on the Methodist circuit riders who traveled throughout the Colonies with the Gospel that half of them died before reaching the age of 33.[6]

When the tireless Methodist preacher Francis Asbury first came to the Colonies in 1771, there were only 600 American Methodists. When he died 45 years later, there were 200,000. One person out of every 40 of the total population in the American colonies was a Methodist, largely because of camp meetings such as Cane Ridge and the circuit riders.[7]

Although some healing and deliverance from evil spirits took place, especially during the preaching of John Wesley and George Whitefield, nevertheless these first Methodists did not want to call too much attention to extraordinary manifestations, fearing that they would distract from their main purpose of converting—or reconverting—the masses to Christianity. So healing continued on, but it remained in the background.

In human terms it was as if, for centuries, God had been trying to reach Christian churches by touching a leader here or there, but the official authorities never seemed to get the point. We might surmise that, finally (putting it in human terms), in the twentieth century God's patience seems to have been exhausted. This time He started so many conflagrations in so many places that no one has yet been able to put them out.

And then—was it by coincidence?—the full Pentecostal experience, the fire that spread all over the world and could not be put out, began on January 1, 1901.

Topeka, Kansas

It was then that a woman, Agnes Oznam, who was a student in a Bible course directed by Charles Parham in Topeka, Kansas, had a remarkable spiritual experience. His small class had been studying the book of Acts and Agnes felt inspired to pray for the baptism in the Holy Spirit, so she asked Parham to pray for her. As Parham later recalled,

> I laid my hands upon her and prayed. . . . I had scarcely completed three dozen sentences when a glory fell upon her, a halo seemed to surround her head and face, and she began speaking the Chinese language and was unable to speak English for three days.[8]

Again, an out of the way place, unknown people, strangely touched by God.[9]

Parham accepted the validity of Agnes's new, but ancient, Pentecost experience and also taught that tongues was the initial evidence that someone had truly been baptized in the Spirit. He also came up with the theory that Christian missionaries didn't need to learn foreign languages. All they had to do was to preach in tongues and everyone would understand, as on that initial day of Pentecost when everyone—Parthians, Medes and Elamites (see Acts 2:9)—understood what Peter was saying. Parham had some success preaching about this new Pentecost and then moved to Houston, Texas, where he started another Bible class.

The next small step in this major outpouring occurred there in Houston when an itinerant black preacher named William Seymour asked Parham if he could attend the class. Parham was, however, a Ku Klux Klan sympathizer and refused to allow Seymour to sit inside his classroom. As a Christian, though, he realized that he could hardly refuse someone a chance to hear the Gospel, so he allowed Seymour to sit outside the classroom building, with the window open so he could listen in. (On rainy days Seymour was allowed to sit inside, but outside the classroom, in the hallway with the door half open!)

Through Parham's teaching Seymour became convinced of the reality of a present-day experience of the baptism of the Spirit, accompanied by the gift of tongues, although he himself had not yet experienced it. Shortly afterward, Seymour received an invitation from Sister Hutchins, a Baptist evangelist who had rented a storefront church, to go west and preach in Los Angeles. And so Seymour ended up fulfilling his lifelong dream of preaching, even though it was halfway across the country.

Azusa Street

From this small beginning came the celebrated Azusa Street revival, which is largely credited for igniting the great twentieth-century Pentecostal explosion.

People who met William Seymour described him as quiet and unassuming, somewhat disheveled in appearance, blind in one eye. Soon he got into a theological dispute with Sister Hutchins (he believed speaking in tongues was more important than she did), and he found himself locked out of even Sister Hutchins's small home church. Undaunted, he continued to organize worship meetings in the simple homes of black domestic servants. More and more people started to attend his services and on April 9, 1906, "the power fell" (as Pentecostals say), and Seymour himself began praising God in unknown tongues.

Almost immediately, the crowds started pouring in and Seymour and his little group had to find new quarters. They settled on a former church that had most recently been converted into a livery stable and there, on April 14 in the humble surroundings at 312 Azusa Street, the new meetings began. With no attempt at publicity, no handbills, no ads, Los Angeles soon was abuzz with excitement about what was happening. A pulpit was constructed with piled-up shoeboxes, and the church's seats were formed of planks laid across empty shipping boxes.[10]

It was the familiar story: God starting something new among the poor and uneducated, on the wrong side of town.

The meetings were filled with emotion, singing and shouting, and people were heard praying in tongues. But what was even more amazing, for that day, was the interracial leadership and the fact that blacks and whites, men and women, were praying and worshiping together. Many visitors were impressed at seeing the Spirit break down the traditional racial barriers, while others were disgusted by the unusual spectacle. Soon newspaper reporters arrived and proceeded to describe whites and blacks mingling in a "religious frenzy" and carrying on "mad orgies."[11]

Nevertheless, many visitors attracted by curiosity, who had come to ridicule the proceedings, ultimately stayed to pray and were deeply touched. Like so many media events, an immediate furor was created, but Azusa Street was different in that its influence soon spread throughout the United States, especially the South (the "Bible Belt"), and it quickly flowed overseas.

Although the Azusa Street revival lasted only three and a half years, it launched the entire Pentecostal Movement and resulted in the formation of the classical Pentecostal churches, such as the Assemblies of God. Azusa Street truly was the mustard seed that grew into a mighty tree!

Visitors thronging to Azusa Street included many pastors, but most of these ministers, black and white, were from poor, struggling Holiness churches. The established churches, if they noticed at all what was going on, poured scorn on the "weird babble of tongues." Only four days after the opening of the Azusa Street Mission, the city of San Francisco experienced its famous earthquake, followed by a devastating fire that destroyed much of the city. For revivalists, the earthquake seemed a harbinger of the Last Days, and this led some desperate Christians to see Azusa Street as a last forlorn hope for the human race.

Seymour had to face the expected opposition from the outside, but ironically, he suffered more from the internal conflict in his own group that so often harms Christian renewal projects (take, for example, the splitting of the Franciscans which started even before Francis of Assisi died!).

To take one example of Seymour's unexpected opposition, Charles Parham, whose Bible study in Kansas had been the spark that kindled the Pentecostal renewal and who had been Seymour's teacher in Texas, decided to visit Los Angeles and see what his former student was doing. Seymour graciously asked Parham to preach, and he used this precious opportunity to lambaste Seymour. Parham's Ku Klux Klan prejudices were excited and he was aghast to see how the racial barriers between black and white were being broken down. He later wrote that he had seen people "crowded together around the altar like hogs, blacks and whites mingling; this should be enough to bring a blush of shame to devils, let alone angels, and yet this was all charged to the Holy Spirit."[12]

Parham was also critical of what he saw as emotional excesses, the historical accompaniments of powerful moves of the Spirit that are regarded by staid Christian observers as being hysterical and uncouth. Once again, poor people from the lower classes seem to be more open to a religion that is not controlled in the head. Going back to St. Peter at the first Pentecost, Christian leaders have had to defend themselves for being unlearned and overemotional. Seymour's elders had to respond to Parham's outbursts by asking the white minister to leave and never come back.

Then, as a further blow, the two women who edited Seymour's little magazine stole his mailing list and absconded with it to Portland, Oregon, where they started their own healing mission. This meant that Seymour's access to contributions dried up.

The last blow fell when William Durham, one of Seymour's early white supporters, revisited Los Angeles and Seymour asked him to preach. Like Parham, Durham launched into an attack on Seymour's ministry. The rationale for the attack was theological, but the idea of white leaders serving under black leadership may have been the real reason. Again, because Durham persisted in his negative stance, Seymour had to lock Durham out of his makeshift church.

Later, in 1914, when Durham was an influence in the formation of the Assemblies of God, he helped establish the ruling that white pastors could not serve under blacks. As a result, the first major Pentecostal denomination became all white in its leadership. As a reaction to this racial prejudice, black pastors were forced into forming their own churches, the most notable being the Church of God in Christ. The Azusa Street Mission had been famous for breaking down the racial barriers, and already, eight years down the line, the old walls were up again.

Seymour had to endure all these bitter times, and it forced him to change his mind in several key areas. He had begun by agreeing with Parham that the gift of tongues was the basic evidence for being baptized in the Spirit—a teaching that still characterizes the Assemblies of God. But then when he realized that so many white Pentecostal leaders were able to pray in tongues while still looking down on blacks, he became convinced that the best sign of the Holy Spirit was destruction of racial barriers.

The white Pentecostals disagreed with Seymour and agreed with the predominant American culture that looked down on blacks. The white pastors decided to stick to their emphasis on tongues and forget about breaking down racial barriers. Gradually, Seymour reviewed his original position and came to the moderate conclusion that tongue-speaking was only one among many charismatic gifts. Eventually, he ended up teaching that the most important evidence for being a Christian was manifesting the fruits of the Spirit, such as love, joy, peace and longsuffering.

As a result of all these disputes, combined with Seymour's increasing weariness, fewer and fewer visitors came to Azusa Street. The congregation gradually became all black. Finally, the little mission was torn down and Seymour slipped away, out of notice until he died in 1922. Today the site of Azusa Street is a parking lot.

And yet, in those brief, vibrant years, the Azusa Street Mission had a profound impact on the future history of Christianity. It was like an explosion. Within six months of Azusa Mission's founding, 38 missionaries had already spread out—first to major cities in the United States, but then across the world—to such distant destinations as Egypt, Norway and South Africa.

Reacting against the formality of organized religion, these Pentecostals could no longer be contained by the established churches. As Harvey Cox has observed, religious conservatives dug in, maintaining their ecclesiastical status quo, insisting on their unchangeable doctrines and on a divinely established hierarchy, while liberals tried to reach the modern world by being socially relevant, all the while losing members. The Pentecostals, on the other hand,

> rebelled against creeds but retained the mystery. They abolished hierarchies but kept ecstasy. They rejected both scientism *and* traditionalism. They returned to the raw inner core of human spirituality and thus provided just the new kind of "religious space" many people needed.[13]

Perhaps the greatest difference between Pentecostalism and traditional religion is that traditional religious services stress teaching and *belief in the unseen* presence of God (as, for example, in the sacraments), while Pentecostals stress having an *experience* of Jesus and the Holy Spirit. When people actually experience God, they usually also experience deep emotion. Sometimes they respond in tears as they are convicted of sin; at other times, they feel great joy flowing over into laughter as they personally sense how much God loves them. Expectant prayer for healing and deliverance is an essential feature of Pentecostal belief, as the believers trust in God's love for them to remove the obstacles of sickness and oppression from their lives.

Since so much of Pentecostalism is based on God's actually doing something transformational in people's lives, the sermons often contain stories and testimonies rather than an emphasis on doctrine and moral exhortation. Pentecostal preachers encourage listeners to trust that God will move in similar, extraordinary ways to touch and transform their own lives. As we know, this kind of preaching has great popular appeal, and most of the famous televangelists today are exponents of healing miracles.

Many pastors who were searching for more meaning, and for more of God in their own ministries, came long distances to Azusa Street and were deeply touched. Upon returning to their churches, they tried to communicate and share what had happened to them. Some entire churches accepted this new manifestation. After staying a few weeks at Azusa Street in 1907, several leaders of the Church of God in Christ accepted the new experience and this church has, since then, become the largest black Pentecostal denomination.

Another newly formed Holiness denomination, the Church of God, became Pentecostal when its highest officer, A. J. Tomlinson, was listening to a sermon by a minister who had just visited Azusa Street. Tomlinson was so moved that he fell out of his chair and crumpled up in a heap. He then received the baptism in the Spirit and, according to his own testimony, spoke in ten different languages. Most of the ministers in this new denomination also sought the Pentecostal experience and proceeded to form the Church of God of Cleveland, Tennessee, which is still growing.

Other pastors—the majority—were not so fortunate and were expelled from their churches. These men gathered together—356 of them—in April 1914 to form the Assemblies of God, which has now grown to be the largest Pentecostal denomination in the world. Unfortunately, as we have mentioned, the initial breaking down of racial barriers was soon overwhelmed by the cultural bias of the day and the Assemblies pastors were all white and all male. In 1994, however, their spiritual descendants repented at the "Memphis Miracle," when four thousand leaders assembled to ask forgiveness for the eighty-year-old division between black and white churches, and to pray for reconciliation between the two groups while washing each other's feet.

As for feminine leadership, women have always been foremost in spreading the Pentecostal message. Even though most of the early Pentecostal leaders had come out of evangelical churches, which stressed male headship and forbade female preachers, women nevertheless experienced an immediate improvement in their situation. For one thing, especially in the Third World, men who had been baptized in the Spirit became more responsible fathers to their families and more loving to their wives. In Latin cultures the power of the Spirit seemed to moderate "machismo," as men stopped spending their wages on drink and prostitutes and returned to their homes.

Other women went well beyond this and felt that the Pentecostal experience had endowed them with gifts of preaching and leadership. The most famous of these pioneers was Aimee Semple McPherson, who truly absorbed the Pentecostal conviction that God had broken down the barriers between Jew and Gentile and between male and female.

She took to heart the Pentecostal emphasis on the ministry of laypeople and that everyone, not just clergy, needed to be out there spreading the Good News of the Gospel. (Remember that these were the days when, in the United States, women were still struggling for the right to vote.) In 1923, after spending years preaching revival in tents, McPherson built her own Angelus Temple (which still stands) in Los Angeles. It seated 5,300, and she became the first of a long procession of media stars in the Pentecostal Movement. Crowds of people flocked to hear her speak and to have her pray for their healing.

She was perhaps the first famous healing evangelist, and eventually she even founded her own denomination, the International Church of the Foursquare Gospel. By the time she died (1944), the denomination numbered 410 churches with 29,000 members. By 1995 the Foursquare Church had grown to more than 25,000 churches with 1,700,000 members in 74 countries.

Since most of the Pentecostal churches were free of established traditions, they felt liberated enough to experiment and try new forms of services. In some sense the Pentecostal scene looked chaotic, with new denominations springing up, with dissension among leaders and with some "prophets" predicting the date for the end of the world.

But it was precisely the fact that most of this renewal took place among the theologically illiterate, those who were not already seminary-trained in the "proper" way to perform services, that helped make it so vibrant. Furthermore, Pentecostal renewal seems to have been most successful when it took place far away from denominational leadership: in places like Cane Ridge, Kentucky; Azusa Street, Los Angeles; and Topeka, Kansas. God was moving, far away from Boston and New York, where seminary professors did not even realize that these dramatic events were going on.

And when the movement did draw attention, it was seen as beneath serious notice. These were ignorant people—tagged as "holy rollers" and "snake handlers." They had no clout. We are reminded again of the religious leaders' amazement at Peter and John's assurance, "considering they were uneducated laymen" (Acts 4:13, JB).

Aimee Semple McPherson stands out as one whose services were innovative and creative. In one Sunday service she rode onto the stage on her motorcycle. In another, she preached from a twenty-foot-high replica of an Easter lily. Harvey Cox describes the symbolic thrust of her emerging one Sunday in a fully operational Trojan horse:

> I can imagine Sister Aimee, emerging from a door in the side of the horse, sword in hand, to subdue the startled Trojans. And I think of the verse in the Acts of the Apostles [Acts 2:17] that anoints both sons and daughters as prophets as a kind of theological Trojan horse. Having been dragged into the center of male-dominated Christianity, the door has now opened. And even Homer could never have foreseen what the result would be.[14]

It was as if all the power of the Spirit, pent up for two thousand years, finally burst free of the established churches.

So for the first fifty years of the twentieth century, these fires were spreading all over the land, so many, so far from ecclesiastical rigidity. Eventually, they blazed out of control and the theologians could no longer put them out.

22

CHARISMATIC RENEWAL AND THE THIRD WAVE

Finally, halfway through the twentieth century, the fire of the Spirit leapt over the wall of respectability, as it were, and began to touch the middle management of the established churches.

Take one example. In 1952, the Reverend Tommy Tyson, a young, successful Methodist pastor, experienced the baptism in the Holy Spirit accompanied by praying in tongues. The elders of his church encouraged him to resign his pastorate—which he did; but his bishop wisely encouraged him to stay within his denomination—which he did until his death (2002).

National publicity for this new version of renewal burst out a few years later (1959) when Dennis Bennett, an Episcopal rector in Van Nuys, California, had the experience of being baptized in the Spirit accompanied by praying in tongues. This time the religious news reached the pages of *Time* and *Newsweek*. (Fr. Bennett wrote up his Pentecostal journey in his well-known autobiography, *Nine O'Clock in the Morning*.)[1] Similar to Tommy Tyson, he was forced to resign his parish position in California, but he resurfaced in another diocese in Seattle, Washington, as a pastor. He remained a faithful Episcopa-

199

lian but was bold about sharing his Pentecostal experience and was responsible for leading many other ministers and laypeople into the same experience.

Soon the Spirit had struck into the heart of every denomination—Presbyterian, Lutheran, Mennonite, Baptist. Then in 1967, the Spirit, at the famous Duquesne weekend (February 18, 1967) touched the hearts of a number of young Roman Catholic leaders.[2] Soon, so many ministers, priests and laypeople had experienced the power of the Spirit and had organized renewal groups, that by the 1970s and 1980s almost every denomination was holding an annual charismatic conference.

Many of them, too, were rather large. The Roman Catholic renewal group, for example, met annually at the University of Notre Dame, and for several years in the mid-1970s, 35,000 people filled the football stadium. In spite of warnings by Pentecostals such as David Wilkerson that the ecclesiastical leaders would pull the rug out from under these charismatic groups, as had happened so often in the past, most of these groups were tolerated and often accepted.

Again, taking the Roman Catholic Church as an example of this extraordinary outpouring, an international conference took place in Rome in 1975 in the famous St. Peter's Basilica. Some ten thousand people came from all over the world. The final Mass was celebrated by Pope Paul VI, who gave a kind of official approval to Catholic charismatic renewal. By this time Leon Cardinal Suenens had become the pope's advisor in regard to the charismatic renewal. At one point in that concluding Mass, the assembled crowd sang so loudly that they drowned out the Sistine Choir.

This dramatic outpouring of the Spirit in all the mainline churches was accompanied by a renewed experience of all the charismatic gifts—healing and prophecy, in particular. A high point of this remarkable renewal was the interdenominational charismatic meeting held in 1977 at Arrowhead Stadium in Kansas City, Missouri. It was attended by about fifty thousand people and represented almost all the major denominations, as well as many independent Pentecostals.

Shortly afterward, another wave of renewal started up among evangelicals. This has been called the "Third Wave"—the first two waves being the Pentecostal renewal, which started new denominations, and the charismatic renewal, which touched the mainline denominations. In particular, John Wimber, a former jazz musician and arranger for the Righteous Brothers, had a conversion experience in Las Vegas. From that point on, he started on a spiritual journey that took him from being an agnostic to becoming a prayer group leader, to becoming a Quaker pastor, to becoming affiliated with Calvary Chapel, and then on to founding the Vineyard Christian Fellowship, which now numbers hundreds of churches and has had a major impact on many parts of the Christian world—England, in particular. Wimber discovered the key relationship between the ministry of healing and evangelism in his restless search for truth and wrote an influential book, *Power Healing*.[3]

Another extraordinary phenomenon in this Third Wave is the great success of the Toronto Airport Christian Fellowship, which in the late 1990s became the number one tourist attraction in Toronto, Canada. Thousands of visitors, including many pastors (in one year, 18 percent of the visitors were pastors), came to see and experience healing, basking in the intense presence of God ("carpet time," they call it). Again, a simple place: in this case, a converted warehouse. Divine healing is a major emphasis at this exciting church, which came out of the Vineyard tradition and is pastored by John and Carol Arnott.

There are too many of these explosions of the Spirit to list them all here. So many new fires are breaking out that they can no longer be counted or contained. The whole phenomenon is fascinating. In some cases the renewal is taking place within established churches and doctrinal lines. In other cases the renewal groups are independent; pastors have started their own churches—some even growing into new denominations—and named themselves bishops when their churches have grown to a sufficient size and prominence.[4]

Throughout the World

So far most of this book has been describing what has been going on in the United States, the United Kingdom and to some extent Europe, but this is only a small part of what is happening today throughout the world. Events in Asia, Africa and Latin America far outstrip in Christian growth what has happened in North America—extraordinary as that is.

In my own experience I remember even as far back as 1978 gathering a team of seven to travel to India. We gave two five-day conferences to a total of four hundred priests and thirteen bishops, culminating in a healing service in Bombay for twenty thousand people. At the end of the service we sent two hundred priests (accompanied by teams of laypeople) into the crowd to pray for the sick.

In fact, the remarkable charismatic renewal in the established churches—Presbyterian, Methodist, Episcopal and Roman Catholic—made it look, for a while, as if those churches might become totally renewed. But this stream, while still flowing in places, now seems generally to have reached a plateau. Although charismatic renewal, including healing, has been more or less accepted—as an example, currently I cannot keep up with the invitations for healing services that are coming from churches from all different denominations—still, to some extent it has been "domesticated."

In many churches that hold Communion services, for example, you will find several lay leaders appointed to pray for the sick at the end of the service. Certainly, this is a big advance, a great change over the way it was fifty years ago. Furthermore, the Order of St. Luke was founded to promote the healing ministry and has been active and successful for half a century, especially among Episcopalians.

Nevertheless, you do not ordinarily see most bishops or district superintendents or ministers openly espousing divine healing. You do not find most traditional non-Pentecostal churches openly encouraging their people who may suffer from a smoking addiction to come to them and receive prayer to be set free. Nor do you hear of leaders in churches that oppose homosexuality offering healing prayer to change the homosexual's orientation; they seem to have accepted the point of view that homosexual orientation does not change.[5] Nor do you hear most leaders speak openly about demonic oppression and the possibility of being freed through deliverance prayer. My own experience leads me to believe that perhaps one out of three Christians—let alone non-Christians—needs to be freed from some form of demonic oppression.[6]

Or take the seminaries: How many offer courses in how to pray for physical (bodily) healing or for inner (psychological) healing—or for deliverance? I have heard of several seminaries that do have such courses, but they are rare. And, is their teaching only theoretical or is it also pastoral and practical? If divine healing is not taught to the future leaders of the Church, the impression given is—necessarily—that it is a side issue and unimportant. Back in the late 1970s, an annual five-day charismatic conference at Steubenville University (Steubenville, Ohio) was held for Roman Catholic priests and deacons. It grew at one point to twelve hundred participants, but it has now fallen off in numbers.

What happened? Although a few bishops and other top leaders became active in charismatic renewal, most of the clergy who actually started praying for healing and deliverance were found, as it were, in "middle-management"—a few priests and ministers. But for whatever reason (perhaps those few were overworked) this number stopped growing.

Another factor in damping down this charismatic renewal has been that the major denominations, by and large, have not considered changing their regular Sunday services or liturgies to include any charismatic dimensions. They go by the book: the Missal or the Book of Common Prayer.

Does in-depth healing fit into regular church services? Must all Sunday services be the same? How does baptism in the Holy Spirit connect with infant baptism or confirmation? Who asks these practical questions and works them out in practice? If someone needs deliverance, when is that arranged? And who can pray for it, when priests and ministers are already overburdened? And how and when do Christians make an adult commitment of their lives to Jesus Christ? Where do young Christians go to find excitement and vitality in a Sunday service? Why are people, in growing numbers, leaving the older, established denominations to join the newer, independent groups that are free to incorporate charismatic dimensions in their worship?

Dr. David Barrett has done comprehensive research on the growth of this astonishing spiritual renewal, and he divides the revival of the charismatic gifts into three waves (as we have done), like the waves hitting a beach flowing in from a mighty ocean. Each builds upon an earlier wave and each is mightier than the last.

The *Pentecostal* wave started to roll in at Azusa Street in 1906. By the year 2000 this wave had grown into 65 million Pentecostals in 740 Pentecostal denominations, including the Assemblies of God and the Church of God in Christ. In this first wave, 90 percent of those who experienced a personal Pentecost were forced to resign from their churches and another 6 percent voluntarily left their parent churches. This led in turn to the formation of many new Pentecostal denominations. In general, their leaders were disenfranchised and angry and saw the established denominations as lost: "Come out from among them!"

The *charismatic renewal* wave was larger than the first wave, with 175 million people in all the major denominations—Catholic and Protestant. Midlevel leadership positions in all these denominations have been permeated by charismatics. These Christians who have had a charismatic experience have mostly stayed (75 percent) within the parent churches to form organizations that host annual conventions, but some 25 percent have left to join other "Spirit-filled" churches or to found independent charismatic churches. These now number around 100,000, loosely organized into 3,700 denominations or other groupings.

The *Third Wave* dwarfs the others. It has now reached the number of 295 million "neo-charismatics," more than the total of Pentecostals and charismatics added together. These Christians have formed 18,810 independent neo-charismatic denominations![7]

Estimates are that this astounding growth will increase worldwide to a total of 811 million by the year 2025. Significantly, 71 percent are non-white. They are Third World (66 percent) rather than First World (32 percent) and most of them are living in poverty.[8]

In a mere hundred years, this number of "neo-Pentecostals" who have experienced the power of the Spirit has grown to such a remarkable extent that it now represents the second largest group of Christians in the world—the first being the Roman Catholics. It outnumbers the total of all the traditional Protestants put together.

And they believe once more in the gift of divine healing.

23

THE NEW FACE
OF CHRISTIANITY

O ne of the features of Christianity today is that religious faith
in many traditional centers of Christianity is struggling. If
you have been to Europe recently, you have probably experienced
this firsthand, compared even with twenty years ago. Visiting London
last year at Christmas time, our family had a hard time finding even a
Christmas card, and the religious section of the bookstores was a tiny
section mainly populated by a few books on spiritualism.

Going beyond the personal to a larger view, 44 percent of the British population no longer claim any religious affiliation (in 2000),
and two-thirds of those 18 to 24 are nonreligious. In Germany, of
the 28 million Protestants, only one million still go to church. In
France, "the eldest daughter of the Church," only 8 percent are still
practicing Catholics.[1] Although there are some bright, vital centers of
Christianity (several of my friends recently spoke at two British youth
rallies totaling 23,000 young people), the general feeling you get is
that Christianity is old and dying. Even the population of tradition-
ally Christian countries is slowly dying out. In Italy and Poland the
birth rate is too low to sustain the present population, and foreign

laborers (frequently non-Christian) are imported to provide workers to keep up the economy.

European and American bishops and theologians, looking at this discouraging situation, are coming up with various strategies to make Christianity relevant to contemporary culture. And yet, what most Christians in the industrial nations are not aware of, is that astonishing church growth is taking place in Africa, Asia and Latin America—in the poor and often oppressed Third World countries.

Here are several notable examples. In Rio de Janeiro in the early 1990s, seven hundred new Pentecostal churches were started in a three-year span. During that same time, two hundred and forty spiritist temples were founded, but just one new Catholic church![2] In China it is estimated there are between twenty and fifty million Christians (since house churches are forbidden, the numbers can only be estimated), and there are more active Christians than in France or England.[3] In Lagos, Nigeria, German evangelist Reinhard Bonnke recently spoke to a gathering of 1.6 million, and there have been reports of a man raised from the dead at his meetings.[4]

Although the largest bloc of Christians is still in Europe (560 million), it is predicted that in a few years, in 2025, Europe's numbers will fall to third place, behind Africa and Asia, which will soon become the main centers of Christianity.[5] In the year 1900 there were only ten million Christians in Africa. By 1965, this number had grown to 75 million, and then to 360 million by 2000![6]

The era of Western Christendom's preeminence is passing away, even in our lifetime, but this historic phenomenon is hardly mentioned in the media. And most Christian leaders in the West are only faintly aware of what is happening. The liberal point of view is that all religious traditions have roughly the same value, so let's stop forcing our culture on them. As a result, even within some Christian denominations, there is an increasing hostility to evangelizing the rest of the world. When they hear about the vast crowds attending religious meetings in Africa, they tend to view the events as "folk religion," akin to superstition. Yet sociologists claim that this worldwide religious movement is perhaps "the most successful social movement of the past century."[7]

The extraordinary thing is that Christianity (at least that part of it that is thriving) has returned to the earliest tradition, the tradition of the first three hundred years that we described in the opening of this book. The salient feature of the early Church was that simple, uneducated poor people underwent an intense experience of the Risen Christ and of the power of the Spirit. This inspired them to go out preaching that the Kingdom of God was at hand. They proceeded to make it happen by healing the sick and casting out evil spirits.

Likewise today, these individuals have already experienced the world of evil spirits as part of the culture in which they have grown up, where shamans and witch doctors once were their spiritual leaders. They think it makes good sense to believe that God sent Jesus Christ to overcome and subdue the power of Satan and the world of demons, whose influence they know only too well. They view the spiritual world of angels and demons as real and not fanciful—a world in which theologians from post-Renaissance times could no longer believe.

As simple people, they are not concerned about the intricacies of theological discussion, the kind of disputes that have occupied the attention of the Church since the fourth century.

They have come to believe and, more than that, to *experience* the Person of the Risen Christ.

Having experienced the Person of Jesus, they proceed to experience the power of the Holy Spirit and all the charismatic gifts enumerated by Paul. Among them, the gift of healing is foremost in freeing people from the infirmities of life in a fallen world. Not that they become totally free of suffering, but they do become free of those weaknesses, addictions, emotional illnesses and even physical sicknesses that prevent them from living a fully joyful human life. In experiencing healing—and oftentimes, deliverance from evil spirits—they come to experience God as being a loving parent, or Jesus as a loving brother, rather than as a distant or punitive judge—the "High God" of the distant heavens in traditional native religions.

If you have ever attended a truly Pentecostal or charismatic worship gathering, you are at once struck by the joy, the vitality and energy, and the vibrancy of the singing and praise that are so often missing from the staid, quiet services of most established churches.

Those who study current philosophical and theological trends recognize that this outpouring of the Spirit is particularly attractive to young people. It draws a "post-modern" generation that is more influenced by experience and by leaders who seem "real" and authentic than by learning doctrines and being loyal to a denomination—the attitude that prevailed fifty years ago. Not that truth is no longer important. But now it must be personally experienced. Truth, "Veritas," is the motto of Harvard, the college I attended, and, coincidentally, is also the motto of the Dominican Order to which I belonged. But in the light of the One who makes His presence known, the search for abstract truth can have only so much relevance. St. Thomas Aquinas, the most famous Dominican theologian, had a vision of the crucified Lord toward the end of his life. Then he said: "Everything I have written until now seems to me like so much straw." After that he wrote no more.

In practical terms, belief in spiritual power seems to make its greatest impact through healing. In Africa today, the churches stand or fall based on their healing success.[8] Christian leaders all over the Third World are tested by power encounters with witch doctors. Just as in the early Church the kingdom of evil is very real. The people know that they have desperate need for God's help to overcome the forces of evil.

The Pentecostal and charismatic churches differ from most of the churches in the older denominations because they believe that God intervenes directly in everyday life. Perhaps this is the reason why Jesus chose poor working people as His first disciples—fishermen who had no difficulty recognizing that they were not self-sufficient. "Blessed are the poor," Jesus said. And yet how successful they are in reaching the masses! In Latin America today the mainline Protestants are middle class; the Pentecostals generally are poor and yet they account for 80 percent of the growth in Protestant churches.[9] They cannot afford medical care so they turn to God to heal their diseases.

I have to admit that I used to be appalled by well-meaning young pastors who, after having their first great religious experience and trying unsuccessfully to share it with their church, would then say something like this: "I'm going to start my own little New Testament church down the street next week." *What pride!* I would think to myself. *Why does he think he can do better than the millions of Christians who have been around for the past two thousand years? Why create one more division in an already fractured Christianity?*

But now I see a possible purpose behind this splitting off. The established leaders seem to defend the status quo and refuse to change. For example, in Africa, converts to Christianity might be told by the missionaries from Europe that witchcraft is just an illusion, a remnant from primitive religion. But to them it is not an illusion; witchcraft works. Reading the life of Jesus in the Bible, they take His words literally. They try casting out evil spirits and find that the method works and people are dramatically and joyously freed.

William Wade Harris is a dramatic example of this. Harris, a black convert to Christianity, a prophet in Liberia, West Africa, began preaching in 1913. When white missionaries told him that witchcraft was just a delusion, Harris rejected their teaching. He had no alternative but to go his own way. Since he knew that fetishes contain spiritual power, he burned them. The story goes that pagan shrines burst into flames when he approached, and their priests fled when he drew near.[10] Many of his followers joined conventional churches, but others founded independent churches that still survive in West Africa.

Africa is home to hundreds of these churches, such as the Aladura churches of Nigeria, which all feature healing prayer. (In fact, in 1974 I was asked to form a team to preach in six cities of Nigeria because the Catholic missionaries had found that, although the people attended Mass on Sunday morning, they would also go to Aladura meetings Sunday night in order to receive the healing and deliverance prayer they were not receiving in the Catholic Church.)

I must note that there are some growing, thriving, traditional denominations in Africa, that have embraced the Spirit's empowerment, especially in healing. These include Anglicanism in Uganda, which now has grown to seven thousand parishes, following the martyrdom of Archbishop Luwum in 1977 by the armed forces of the dictator Idi Amin.[11] Even more explosive has been the growth of the native independent Pentecostal churches, which go by such creative names as the Cherubim and Seraphim Society. (Many of these independent, native-led churches were hastened into existence because the European churches refused to admit blacks into leadership until the past fifty years.)

The Christianity that is succeeding looks massively different from what we find today in the traditional churches of Europe. In this newer—and yet older—version of Christianity, the worship is enthusiastic, creative, spontaneous and supernaturally oriented. All these groups center on a personal relationship with Jesus Christ, an experience of the Holy Spirit's empowering, and an outpouring of God's desire to heal and free our poor wounded humanity—as we have seen throughout this book, the very message of the Gospel.

In all these waves we see a massive reawakening of the healing ministry. The stage is now the entire globe. The Pentecostal explosion is taking place outside Europe—which used to be the center of Christianity—in places where the Pentecostal experience is outside ecclesiastical control.

As we noted, one factor contributing to the spread of the renewal of healing and exorcism was that by the time this huge Pentecostal fire had started, a fire vast enough to attract the attention of the mainline churches, roughly fifty years had passed and too many places and too many people had been reached. The fire could no longer be quenched. At first the fire fell on individuals like Dennis Bennett. Then it happened to individual churches, like the Toronto Christian Airport Fellowship. Then to entire churches, like the Vineyard or the Anglicans of Uganda.

A major factor in this revival has been the rediscovery of the baptism of the Spirit. As we have said, during the first three hundred years after Christ's death, the Church expected that new Christians would receive a Pentecost experience—for instance, they might prophesy or pray in tongues—when they were immersed in the waters of baptism. This belief lasted for four centuries and only gradually died out.

I do not believe that it was just coincidence that a lively experience of the baptism of the Spirit went along with the belief that all Christians were equipped to pray for healing and the casting out of evil spirits. As we have found in our exploration, the power of the Spirit is the dynamic force of God that lies behind the ministry of healing and deliverance. You cannot have one without the other.

The body had lain almost motionless—so inert that some of the greatest thinkers thought that it had died. They could find no pulse.

But now the heart, the Spirit, the fire is back. Once more the Spirit is falling on a waiting humanity—Parthians, Medes and Elamites!

24

WILL WE REMAIN ON THE SIDELINES?

By now you realize that a serious crime has been committed. An essential part of Christianity was nearly killed off—yet some life remained. In the last century, moreover, there have been signs of a major renewal in the power of the Holy Spirit.

But still, Christian practice in most churches today does not reflect authentic first-century Christian tradition. Even stranger, some of the churches most loyal to Scripture have lost an essential part of the Christian life. And they do not even know it.

What is the crime? Simply that the great gift God sent to transform our lives—the "promise," Luke calls it, the Holy Spirit—has mostly been taken away. We maintain our belief in the Holy Spirit; some churches even celebrate a special Feast of Pentecost. But by and large we have neglected the practical part of this new life: how to receive our own personal Pentecost, together with the charismatic gifts we need in order to be transformed into a glorious new creation.

To become like Jesus, we need to experience and display the fruits of the Spirit until we love people with Jesus' own love, see reality as Jesus sees it and reflect all the other traits of Jesus' character, such as joy, peace and patience. To help us do this, Jesus empowers us with the charismatic gifts (some of which are listed in 1 Corinthians 12, such as healing), which help us get rid of the blocks to our becoming new creations and give us the power to overcome demonic opposition and cast out evil spirits.

As Paul describes our situation in Romans 7, we fail to live up to our own God-inspired ideals and, instead, do the very things we hate. Without the help of the Spirit, we cannot live the Christian ideal to the fullest. Two thousand years of history demonstrate that, for the most part, Christians have not been able to live up to the Great Commandment of loving others in the same way He has loved us.

We talk a good game. We believe true doctrine. But most of us have never learned to seek and receive the baptism with the Holy Spirit and to exercise the gifts of the Spirit.

If, according to the main prophecy of John the Baptist (in each of the four gospels), Jesus is the One who baptizes us with the Spirit, why is it that so many Christians do not understand the question "Have you been baptized with the Spirit?" And how is it that, although Paul declares that we need the charismatic gifts of the Spirit to build up the Church, most Christians do not even grasp what the question "Have you received the gift of tongues?" means?

So the heart of the Christian life—the experienced power of the Holy Spirit—is beating but weakly.

God intends for us to live a new life in the Spirit, a living law working from inside to help us become Christlike rather than a law written on stone and working from the outside, motivating us by promising reward and threatening punishment. The inner presence of God, brought to us by the Spirit, is meant to transform us, while the charisms enable us to help others be transformed.

Scripture teaches that the wretched human condition in which we find ourselves requires God's healing power far beyond what we humans can attain on our own. The belief in our need for God's help and power is central to both the Hebrew and the Christian Scriptures, the Old and New Testaments.

Even the Old Testament recounts the occasional example of healing, such as when Naaman, the Syrian general suffering from leprosy, comes to Elijah, who tells him to dip seven times in the muddy Jordan River. Reluctant to obey such a simple command, "since the rivers of

Syria are as good as the Jordan," he finally agrees to the ignominious bath and is marvelously healed. And in the gospels Jesus comes on the scene "with healing in His wings."

In the New Testament we see an explosion of divine healing, as Jesus spent a major part of His time curing the sick and casting out evil spirits.

Nor do the gospels present this work of healing as incidental to Jesus' mission, a signs-and-wonders sideshow. That ministry was an essential part of His work. He proclaimed a new era of human history—"the Kingdom of God has come"—while the kingdom of evil was simultaneously being destroyed. "The reason the Son of God appeared was to destroy the devil's work" (1 John 3:8).

To make this glorious dream come true, Jesus came as our Savior (His primary title), in the power of the Holy Spirit, to free us from our sins, from the influence of evil spirits and from the sickness of body and soul that weighs us down and prevents us from being transformed into the new creations God destined us to become.

Jesus shared with us His own divine power to heal the sick. First He gave it to the Twelve, then to the 72, and finally, since Pentecost, to everyone who chooses to believe and follow Him. The major teaching summing up the entire book of Acts is that God equipped those early followers to do the very same things Jesus did. First they proclaimed to everyone that the Kingdom of God was present, truly in our midst. Then they demonstrated the Kingdom of God by healing the sick and freeing those held captive by evil spirits.

Without the twin ministries of healing and deliverance, our preaching that God's Kingdom is here and that Satan's dominion is being destroyed is hollow.

A Matter of Life or Death

I hope these pages do not come across as strident. If the ministry of healing has indeed almost been destroyed, our response should be great sadness, if not anger, because it has robbed us of a large part of our Christian heritage. We are not just talking about restoring a theoretical doctrine but we are mourning the countless lives lost prematurely because we did not even realize we could help people through our prayers.

When a physician writes that a day may come when doctors can be sued for malpractice if they do not pray for their patients—since prayer is a scientifically proven treatment—what can we say about Christian leaders who do not lay hands on the sick and pray? And if you do not believe in the existence of a demonic realm that influences many people, you can at least recognize that questioning the existence of evil spirits is a relatively recent phenomenon. You owe it to yourself to investigate the evidence for their existence and influence—perhaps even in your own life or in the lives of your loved ones.

Although the past hundred years have seen a great rediscovery of the ministries of healing and deliverance, leaders in many churches still seem reluctant to promote or approve these practices once central to Christian life. As a result, in order to fill the vacuum, many independent charismatic-evangelical churches have sprung up all over the world and are experiencing explosive growth. The mainline churches continue to stand on the sidelines, seemingly more concerned about controlling or domesticating charismatic dimensions of Christianity than in promoting the baptism with the Spirit or the charisms.

Sometimes it is as if the healing ministry is damned by faint praise. I once heard a learned bishop in favor of the renewal say, "Christianity is like an orchestra, everyone playing a different instrument, exercising a different charism, to make up the complete symphony that is the Church. We are glad that you are bringing back some of the instruments we haven't heard for many years to create the full beauty of the orchestra."

In some ways this is a good metaphor. But it says that we have been missing a few things that don't really amount to that much, and it trivializes what is happening. The baptism with the Holy Spirit and the ministries of healing and deliverance are not just restoring the piccolo, flute and bassoon to the orchestra, which can still play without them. They are essential to the life of any church.

If you are trying to help a suicidal woman who was sexually abused as a child and hates herself, she does not just need a deeper insight into truth. What she needs is to be freed from the crippling aftereffects of the abuse. For such people, healing or deliverance is a life-or-death issue. And once you have actually seen the power of God at work transforming a wounded, crippled Christian into a radiant person glad to be alive, you will never be the same.

Until churches connect in-depth healing and deliverance to everyday life, people will continue to drop out and, in some cases, die before their time. It is a start to have a team at the side altar after a church service; but most healing (spiritual as well as physical) requires time and in-depth ministry by knowledgeable prayer ministers. If you have experience dealing with addicts or victims of satanic ritual abuse who have several split-off personalities, you realize how important it is to know Christians with a balanced ministry of healing and deliverance.

Baptism with the Spirit is more than an option allowed in a special prayer meeting in a side room (although many churches do not have even that). Holy Spirit baptism must be explained and made available to everyone in every congregation. Churches that confirm young or new believers must explore the relationship of confirmation to the baptism with the Holy Spirit so that those who are confirmed are also baptized with the Spirit, accompanied by some manifestation of the charismatic gifts, such as prophecy and tongues. Sacramental churches need liturgies in which the charisms are allowed to flow freely in regular church services. Otherwise these more traditional churches will continue to lose many of their members to the newly rising charismatic-evangelical churches.

We are speaking about life or death!

> Those who enter into Christ's being-here-for-us no longer have to live under a continuous, low-lying black cloud. A new power is in operation. The Spirit of life in Christ, like a strong wind, has magnificently cleared the air, freeing you from a fated lifetime of brutal tyranny at the hands of sin and death.
>
> Romans 8:2–3, MESSAGE

Now it is time for us to recognize the depths of our loss and to reverse the process so we can recapture the prize for which Christ Jesus captured us (see Philippians 3:12–14).

To Sum Up

Truly this was the nearly perfect crime.

What was the crime? That the greatest gift Jesus came to give—the Holy Spirit, who enables us to live as new creations—was taken away as an experienced reality in our lives. Many of the charismatic gifts that free us from the obstacles to living transformed lives were also taken away.

Who committed the murder? Nobody was ever accused of an intentional crime—but, for the most part, sincere, holy leaders who thought they were purifying Christianity were the ones who did it.

Who could pray? First, everyone. Then only the ordained. Then even they lost the expectation that healing would take place. A fascinating exception: the kings and queens of England and France who held healing services, but the Royal Touch also died three hundred years ago.

Where did healing still go on? In carefully controlled liturgies with written-out prayers offered by officials. Or, if you were Catholic or Orthodox, at shrines where you might pray for the intercession of a saint.

Why did they think healing might take place? Mostly healing was seen as an occasional sign or wonder, a miracle, in order to prove that something was true, rather than as an everyday occurrence happening simply because God loves His sick children and hates to see them suffer.

When was healing expected to happen? For some, rarely. For others, never. Those in the Catholic and Orthodox traditions expected only an occasional miracle. Among those who followed the Protestant reformers, "Miracles used to happen but no more." Among Christians influenced by scientism, they no longer happen because they never happened in the first place.

Truly healing was dying or, in some churches, was already dead.

If you agree with what I have said so far, you are, I hope, inspired with a desire to do something to restore our lost heritage. Restoration is quite possible. In some countries and churches and groups, it is already gloriously taking place.

You yourself can learn as best you can to receive the empowering of the Spirit and to pray for healing—

for yourself
for your family

for your friends
and, if things are opened up, in your church.[1]

St. Augustine wrote that our hearts are restless until they find their rest in Him. In a day when many notable Christian leaders are trying to find a way to make the Gospel relevant, I propose that authentic Christianity is already relevant. Christianity meets the deepest needs of the human heart—to know God and not just about Him; to know Jesus as Friend and Brother; to experience the power of His Spirit and resurrection in living as new creations, healed of all the evil that holds us down. "I want to know Christ and the power of his resurrection and the fellowship of sharing in his sufferings" (Philippians 3:10).

Perhaps these have been, in many ways, the worst of days. But I am filled with hope that the days to come will be the best of days. Once we rediscover the Source of life, people will beat a path, even a highway, to our door.

APPENDIX

My Discovery of the Baptism with the Holy Spirit

I t was back in 1966 that I first heard about the baptism with the Holy Spirit. In some ways it might seem a short time ago. For me it is a lifetime away.

At the time I was president of the Catholic Homiletic Society, an 1,100-member association (mostly of priests) dedicated to improving preaching in the Roman Catholic Church. I was also the founding editor of its journal *Preaching*. As part of my professional duties, I attended a large speech convention at the Albert Pick Hotel in Chicago.

While I was there, several Protestant ministers introduced me to someone they greatly admired, Jo Kimmel, who taught speech at Manchester College in Indiana. More amazing to them was that she prayed regularly for the sick—who reportedly were healed. Would I like to meet her? Yes. So four of us met for dinner.

What impressed me most about Mrs. Kimmel was her complete naturalness. There seemed to be no division between her ordinary life and her life of prayer. Her conversation about Jesus and how He still healed people was as natural as her talk about her teaching career and her children. I could not help asking myself how many priests I knew who could talk so easily and so unaffectedly about the Lord.

When I questioned her, she showed no self-consciousness in describing the miracles of healing she had seen. And when I expressed surprise about all this happening, she said it was not at all unusual and that there were thousands of people like herself. (At that time I had not met that many, so this statement surprised me.) Then she explained that these remarkable healings had begun after she had received the baptism with the Holy Spirit. As I heard about these experiences, I became hungry to know more.

In the coming months I read some of the books then popular among neo-Pentecostals, such as *They Speak with Other Tongues* by John Sherrill. Happily I was not plagued by the doubts and skepticism that disturb many when they first hear about unfamiliar spiritual topics. In fact, I found myself thirsting to receive the baptism with the Spirit—not in spite of my tradition but because of it.

In many ways I had been prepared for this experience. In my study of spiritual theology, I had learned that *everyone* is called to holiness—which means that we all are called to union with God through the gifts of the Holy Spirit. I had read the lives of the saints and was impressed by the personal knowledge of God they experienced in prayer. I knew about the marvelous accounts of the healings that took place in shrines like Lourdes in France, where thousands of pilgrims visited each day in summer. Why was it, I wondered, that most of us did not receive any of those prayer experiences? Why should miracles occur in only a few places? Why study about those beautiful events if we were not to expect them?

After my ordination in 1956, I had been appointed to teach preaching ("homiletics") in Dubuque, Iowa, in a seminary of the Dominican Order to which I belonged. In those years the gap between the ideal and the real became still more apparent. I was called on to preach conferences about the Christian life and how to reach that ideal. I had to be realistic—not only for myself but for others—that everyone was called on to achieve a deep spiritual union with God but that only a few seemed to reach it.

Spiritual writers offered the explanation that most Christians were not generous enough, that they had simply given up carrying their crosses. In the search for God there were deserts and dark nights of the soul to traverse. Somewhere in this emotional desolation, the aspiring Christian would lay down his cross and start hankering for creature comforts. The answer always given was "Carry your cross unstintingly and don't seek another. Keep carrying it and eventually you will be rewarded, even though it may not be in this life. Above all, don't give up. Just be more generous and accept your suffering."

For eight years I accepted this explanation: lack of generosity for spiritual failures. But I discovered when preaching to communities of sisters, many of whom had been striving for years to become holy, that it simply was not true. I could not tell them that they were not generous or that they had not carried their crosses faithfully. If anything they were too generous; they were working too hard. To be sure, many of them were deeply joyful, deeply holy. But some were struggling, some unhappy. How to explain it? There must be other explanations for what was missing. How do we achieve the joy-filled Christian life that the Gospel speaks about?

The question was insistent: If everyone is called to joyful holiness, how was I to speak about this in a practical way? So I kept searching for new ways of preaching. It wasn't a search for gimmicks; it was a search for content, for reality.

To be frank, I really did not find anything very practical. I prepared sermons on prayer and sermons on love, but still there was this gap—a gap that I found existed in the lives of many priests and ministers, whether they were conscious of it or not.

Like many priests in the early '60s, I began to look for practical assistance from the field of psychology. I began to read authors like Erich Fromm (*The Art of Loving*) and gained many good insights. When you got right down to it, they seemed more practical than most of the devotional books I had read on Christian love. As a result of my desire to meet people's needs, I found myself injecting more and more psychology into my sermons and conferences.

These conferences seemed highly successful. At the end of several high school retreats, the students simply did not want to go home. They found that the usual cliques were breaking down and that old animosities and hatreds were being healed by the spirit of love engendered in the group. This seemed a great improvement over the old-style retreat in which the preacher stood up to speak to a captive audience in the high school gymnasium.

I realized we had come up with something new and successful in retreat format and content, something that was working. Yet at the same time I realized that my basic source of inspiration was not the

Gospel but psychology. My retreat could perhaps have been put on still more successfully by trained group dynamics experts.

While I wondered about this, many other priests in my situation were asking similar questions. Were we simply becoming counselors? Were priests just fulfilling a variety of functions that could just as well be performed by someone else? If we had Ph.D.s in counseling or psychology, could we do a better job than we had been doing? The answer seemed to be yes. But if so, did you need to be a priest to carry on the work that is actually most helpful to people?

About that time, many of my best friends were leaving the priesthood. Some had come to identify themselves primarily as teachers or counselors. And these were not misfits; some were our best men. So I was forced to ponder not simply the matter of effective preaching but the very roots of everything. What did it mean to be a Christian?

It was my very experience as a counselor and confessor that prepared me to understand the need for the power given by the Holy Spirit. Simply because I was a sympathetic listener, all kinds of hurting people came to me for spiritual direction. I did not try to go it alone but worked in conjunction with psychiatrists and psychotherapists. They certainly helped. But the truth was, most patients were being helped to cope with their problems without being healed.

Why was it that the people who were hurting the most seemed to be the ones that no one—neither a psychiatrist nor anyone else—could really help? If Christianity is the good news of being saved, why do some people have a head start while others seem hopeless from the very beginning? They would say, "Well, God may love *you* but He certainly doesn't love *me*. Look at me and my miserable history. I'm living proof." Some would actually ask, "You think I'm hopeless, don't you? I'm never going to get better, am I?"

Deep down I would think to myself, *I don't want to believe they are truly hopeless. But humanly speaking they certainly are.* It was as if there was a determinism in the world conflicting with the message of Jesus—that He came to proclaim release to the captives and to help the lame to walk. He came to the poorest of the poor, the outcasts, the prostitutes, those who had sold out to the Romans. These were the people Jesus loved.

And it was as if there was a power in Jesus and His followers that was missing in my life. At the time it did not surprise me that I could not do the works that Jesus did—even though He had said, "I tell you the truth, anyone who has faith in me will do what I have been doing. He will do even greater things than these" (John 14:12). These thoughts left me with a vague but real sense of something missing. Add to this a sense of urgency arising from my best friends' leaving the ministry, as well as from my desire to find the depth needed to preach the Gospel. Did I have good news to offer the sick, as Jesus did—the good news of healing? Or was I merely confined to offering good advice?

That was why, in 1966, when I heard that there were people who prayed for healing, it made a great deal of sense to me. Maybe this was what was missing in my life that would put it all together. I was determined to investigate the baptism with the Spirit, even though at that time I had heard of no Catholics who knew about this phenomenon.

I asked the question any Catholic would have: What is this baptism with the Spirit, if I had already received the Holy Spirit in baptism, confirmation and ordination? But in the people I met who testified that they had received this experience, I saw the fruits of the Spirit: love, joy and peace. It radiated from their eyes. They were speaking of an experience I could not contradict (nor did I want to) because it held great hope of filling what was missing in our lives. Had not the great spiritual writers said that union with God could come only as a gift? And to receive a gift, we need only to ask, rather than strive to achieve it on our own.

The people I met spoke about gifts of the Spirit—the same "charismatic" gifts I could identify by name, having read about them in Paul's first letter to the Corinthians, as well as in the theological works I had studied. As they described an experience, I could almost see the page on which I had read about such a thing in the life of some saint.

In the Rule of the Dominican Order to which I belonged, it was set down that we should imitate St. Dominic, who always was speaking either to or about God. But I had discovered Protestant friends living out that ideal that seemed too strict and rigid for many of us Dominicans—and they were doing it freely, without any particular rules. Led by an interior movement of the Spirit, they seemed to want to talk about Jesus—not about the historical Jesus but about a Friend. I saw no divergence between the ideal I had always held as a Catholic and the experiences of my Protestant friends.

The following summer, in August 1967, Mrs. Kimmel sponsored me to attend a mammoth retreat called a "Camp Farthest Out" (CFO) in Maryville, Tennessee. My hope in going was to receive the baptism with the Spirit.

When I arrived I was surprised to find that eight hundred people had come to spend six days hearing three sermons a day with prayer interspersed. What struck me most as a teacher of preaching was that all three speakers (the Reverend Tommy Tyson, the Reverend Derek Prince and Mrs. Agnes Sanford) spoke for at least an hour, yet the audience did not tire of listening. In fact, the entire crowd seemed ready to pay attention for another hour.

I realized I must be hearing the gift of inspired preaching that I had talked about in my homiletics course. One of the traditional signs of predestination given by St. Thomas Aquinas, I remembered, was that the person would *gladly* listen to the Word of God—something we had not always seen in our own parishes, in which the people were often glad for a brief sermon. In those days, when I was invited to a Catholic church as a guest preacher, the pastor would sometimes caution me, "You know, we appreciate short sermons here."

Another thing impressed me—the way these hundreds of people were talking about their spiritual experiences in the most natural way. Our Catholic retreats were governed by a rule of silence so that retreatants were not distracted by idle talk. But here was talk that was not a distraction. These people had a deep inner desire, whether there were rules or not, to talk about the things of God.

Not being sure theologically how the baptism with the Spirit related to baptism and confirmation, I could still see that its effects on people's lives were impressive. I decided that I, too, wanted to experience it. Even if it meant my feeling like a fool, I was ready to take the plunge in the midst of all these Protestants, only two of whom I knew! I made an appointment to pray in a small group for the baptism with the Spirit.

This small group prayed with great fervor for five of us who were seeking, but I received no interior experience. When I voiced my disappointment, they asked if I had prayed in tongues. When I answered no, they asked me if I would like to. I said yes, and proceeded to pray fluently in something that sounded like Russian. Yet it seemed as if I was making up the language on my own, so I was still disappointed. I had not been looking for a particular gift but for a deeper experience of Christ, which I knew was at the center of it all. So while the group congratulated me for having received the Holy Spirit, I felt frustrated and confused.

One Lutheran minister threw his arms around me, weeping. "I can see now that even a Catholic priest can receive the Spirit!" he exclaimed.

In the midst of this confusion, I went to the dining hall and happened to stand next to Agnes Sanford, one of the three speakers. As an Episcopalian, sensitive to my religious background, she asked me how my prayer for the baptism with the Spirit had gone. I told her about my disappointment.

"Well, frankly," she responded, "I had the feeling that your group should not pray for you as they usually do, as if you didn't have the Holy Spirit and were receiving the Spirit for the first time. I think it would be better to pray for you for a release of the Spirit and the charismatic gifts that are already in you through baptism, confirmation and ordination."

That made a lot of sense to me.

So the next evening after supper, Mrs. Sanford and two other friends prayed over me that I might receive this unfolding of the Spirit and the release of all the gifts. As she prayed, she shared a prophecy that the Lord would work through me in bringing healing prayer back to the Catholic Church. When she finished the prayer, all four of us were overcome by a wave of laughter. It was as if a spring of joy had welled up from within me, the joy of the Holy Spirit. Wave upon wave of joy engulfed me. We all laughed together, not hysterically but because we were all filled with joy in the presence of God.

It was in this way—a way that seemed just right and suited for me—that I was baptized with the Holy Spirit. It happened in a way I had not planned but I believe God chose and arranged. (Agnes Sanford described the incident in her autobiography, *Sealed Orders*.) Providentially Mrs. Sanford was there to know how best to pray for me. Through her wisdom I was able to understand what was happening; and through that understanding my experience has helped hundreds of ministers and priests open up to the release of the Spirit.

For many of us, the Spirit had been there all the time but was somehow quenched or bottled up. The baptism with the Spirit is a release of the Spirit. (After all, Peter and the other disciples had the Spirit in some measure before Pentecost.)

I have found since then, in praying for many Christian leaders, that ordinarily the baptism with the Spirit is a peaceful experience. For some it is overwhelming, and a manifest change takes place immediately. For most ministers and priests, perhaps, the change is gradual and takes place mainly in the area of their ministry. I have found, too, that Christians who do not receive any obvious experience of the Spirit are often those who are bound by inner sorrow or hurt (and can profit by prayer for healing). Others have grown used to such a restrained, disciplined style of life that they are not free to respond to all the ways the Spirit wants to express God's love and power in our lives.

The change in my own life has been tremendous. Healing and casting out evil spirits really do accompany the preaching of the Good News. I find that people today are hungering to hear not just about doctrines but about Jesus and the Spirit and to meet their reality in their lives. Back in 1964 the total time of talks given on a weekend retreat would have been about three hours. Now we need a team to meet a demanding schedule that include talks, discussion and, above all, prayer, which altogether amount to about twelve hours in a day.

Above all I have found that we are now able to help those very people we once thought were nearly hopeless. Through prayer, real miracles of healing take place—physical healings and, above all, spiritual and psychological ones. We have found that homosexuals who desire to change their orientation can be changed through prayer. Healings of alcoholism and drug addiction are common.

Those phenomena I once regarded as a great but rarely achieved ideal I now see as a matter of course. We have experienced the joy of seeing the lives of Christians—especially leaders such as priests and ministers—completely renewed and transformed. Typical of the letters I receive is the following:

Dear Francis,
Yesterday I was going to write thanking you for giving the greater part of a day to [name], but this morning I can't find words adequate. She wrote me, and for the first time in four years she is *alive*! After suffering so helplessly and so long with her, I can scarcely contain my joy this morning. God has brought about a transformation.

Seeing lives transformed by God's Spirit gives us the reason for the hope that we have (see 1 Peter 3:15). All of us who have experienced the Spirit's transforming power now realize that preaching the Gospel message has changed. It used to be like giving good advice. But now it means proclaiming Good News.

NOTES

Chapter 1: The Nearly Perfect Crime

1. Louis Evely, *The Gospels Without Myth* (New York: Doubleday, 1970), 25.

2. Larry Dossey, M.D., *Prayer Is Good Medicine* (San Francisco: HarperCollins, 1996), 66.

3. By *deliverance*, I mean the freeing of people from the power of evil spirits. The word *exorcism* could be used, but it has been associated in people's minds with the formal rite used only by priests in the Roman Catholic Church and has acquired too narrow a meaning to be helpful here. Among many books on this subject of deliverance, I have also written one: *Deliverance from Evil Spirits: A Practical Manual* (Grand Rapids: Chosen, 1995).

4. Gabriele Amorth, *An Exorcist Tells His Story* (San Francisco: Ignatius Press, 1999), 54–55.

Chapter 2: There Has to Be More!

1. Not her real name.

2. William Glasser, M.D., *Reality Therapy: A New Approach to Psychiatry* (New York: Harper & Row, 1965), 8–9.

Chapter 3: Our Long Lost Inheritance

1. Some other translations say "sinful nature," "compulsions of selfishness" and "self-indulgence."

Chapter 4: "And His Name Shall Be Called . . ."

1. The name *John* means "Yahweh is gracious."

2. My friend Tommy Tyson used to say that since *Bar Jona* means "Son of John," or Johnson, from now on we might call Peter "Rocky Johnson"!

3. Peter quotes from Isaiah 61:1, the text Jesus used when He first began His ministry (see Luke 4:18–19).

Chapter 5: How Did Jesus See His Mission?

1. Charles H. Talbert, *Reading Luke* (New York: Crossroad, 1992), 57. Talbert summarizes Jesus' first sermon, as Luke describes it, inaugurating his ministry: " . . . in 4:16–30 the evangelist gives a programmatic statement of Jesus' ministry—and by extension, the ministry of the church—as one empowered by the Holy Spirit, involving not only preaching but also healing and exorcism, and moving outwards to touch the whole world."

2. N. T. Wright, *The Challenge of Jesus* (Downers Grove, Ill.: InterVarsity Press, 1999), 39.

3. William Barclay, *The Gospel of Matthew*, vol. 2, rev. ed. (Philadelphia: Westminster Press, 1975), 28.

4. 1 Maccabees 2:21–38. The two books of Maccabees are included in the Catholic Bible and are listed under the Apocrypha in Protestant Bibles. They show us what Jewish beliefs were just 165 years before Jesus' birth. It is also significant that the Jewish Feast of Dedication, otherwise known as the Feast of Lights, is based on the cleansing of the Temple by the Maccabee brothers. The lighting of the celebrated Menorah, the nine-branched candlestick, takes place in these days. This feast, also known as Chanukah or Hanukkah, comes in the winter and is celebrated as a counterpart to Christmas. In John 10:22–23 we see Jesus going to Jerusalem to celebrate this feast.

5. 2 Maccabees 7:1–5.

Chapter 6: Basic Christian Preaching

1. N. T. Wright, "The Challenge of the Kingdom," in *The Challenge of Jesus*, 34–53.

Chapter 7: The Baptism with the Holy Spirit

1. Kilian McDonnell and George T. Montague, *Christian Initiation and Baptism in the Holy Spirit: Evidence from the First Eight Centuries*, 2d ed. (Collegeville, Minn.: Liturgical Press, 1994), 310.

2. See also Matthew 3:13–17 and Mark 1:9–11.

3. On this subject you might read Harvey Cox's *Fire from Heaven: The Rise of Pentecostal Spirituality and the Reshaping of Religion in the Twenty-First Century* (Reading, Mass.: Addison-Wesley, 1995); and Philip Jenkins's *The Next Christendom: The Coming of Global Christianity* (New York: Oxford University Press, 2002).

4. Dallas Willard states that the Gospel as preached today is often just "sin management" and does not deal with the transformation that Jesus preached. See chapter 2 in *The Divine Conspiracy* (New York: Harper Collins, 1998).

Chapter 8: Ministry with Power: The News Spreads

1. Marc Bloch, "The Royal Miracle during the Wars of Religion and the Absolute Monarchy," in *The Royal Touch* (New York: Dorset Press, 1989), 177–213.

Chapter 9: The Spirit Flourishes: The First 325 Years

1. André Hamman, *Baptism: Ancient Liturgies and Patristic Texts* (Staten Island, N.Y.: Alba House, 1967), 9.

2. Kilian McDonnell and George T. Montague, *Fanning the Flame: What Does Baptism in the Holy Spirit Have to Do with Christian Initiation?* (Collegeville, Minn.: Liturgical Press, 1991), 16.

3. Ibid.

4. Ibid., 17.

5. McDonnell and Montague, *Christian Initiation and Baptism in the Holy Spirit.*

6. McDonnell and Montague, *Fanning the Flame*, 23.

7. For more information on receiving the baptism with the Spirit, I suggest reading Dennis Bennett's *Nine O'Clock in the Morning* and *The Holy Spirit and You.*

8. The New Testament, as we have it, comprising 27 books, did not win general acceptance until the fourth century.

9. Evelyn Frost, *Christian Healing* (London: A.R. Mowbray, 1940), 97.

10. From Arnobius, *Against the Heathen*, in Frank C. Darling, *Biblical Healing: Hebrew and Christian Roots* (Boulder, Colo.: Vista Publications, 1989), 160–61.

11. Origen, *Against Celsus*, vii, 4, 17.

12. Frost, *Christian Healing*, 58.

13. Tertullian, *De Spectaculis*, par. 29.

14. Ramsay MacMullen, *Christianizing the Roman Empire: A.D. 100–400* (New Haven and London: Yale University Press, 1984).

15. The word *supernatural* is not so widely used among theologians today because they wish to indicate that God is at work in all of creation. This is laudable, and yet there is a purpose in using the word *supernatural* to indicate something that happens beyond the limits of what we know about our ordinary human powers and medical science.

16. Justin Martyr, *Apology II—to the Senate*, vi., in Morton T. Kelsey, *Psychology, Medicine and Christian Healing* (San Francisco: Harper & Row, 1988), 108.

17. In his commentary on 1 Corinthians.

18. MacMullen, *Christianizing the Roman Empire*, 22.

19. Ibid., 27.

20. Ibid., 28.

21. MacMullen, *Christianizing the Roman Empire.*

22. Talbert, *Reading Luke*, 56–57.

Chapter 10: The Church Unplugs the Power

1. If you would like to understand this extraordinary movement, I would encourage you to read *The Next Christendom: The Coming of Global Christianity* by Philip Jenkins. The

total members of these new groups now outnumber the total group of traditional Protestants worldwide. Jenkins calls it "the New Christianity," which is really "the Old Christianity," a return to the central elements of traditional Christianity.

Chapter 11: Forgotten Motives: Compassion and Witness to the Truth

1. Francis MacNutt, "Having to Say No," in *The Power to Heal* (Notre Dame, Ind.: Ave Maria Press, 1977), 111–20.

Chapter 12: The Major Decline: Plato and the Pagans

1. It reminds us of the proverbial frog who is placed in a pot of water that is heated so gradually that the frog doesn't even know that it is being boiled to death until it is too late to jump.

2. *Story of a Soul: The Autobiography of St. Thérèse of Lisieux*, 3rd ed. (Washington, D.C.: ICS Publications, 1996).

3. Ibid., 210–11.

4. John T. Noonan Jr., *Contraception: A History of Its Treatment by the Catholic Theologians and Canonists* (New York: Mentor-Omega Books, 1965), 187.

5. "Let Him Carry His Cross Daily," in *Healing* (1974; reprint, Notre Dame, Ind.: Ave Maria Press, 1999), 61–70.

6. See chapters 10 and 11.

Chapter 13: Caught in Transition: St. Augustine

1. St. Augustine's *The City of God*, 450, in Kelsey, *Psychology*, 147.

2. Augustine, *City of God*, XXII.8, 1954, 445, in Kelsey, *Psychology*, 146.

3. Possidius, "Life of St. Augustine," 29, in *Early Christian Biographies* (1952), as quoted in Kelsey, *Psychology*, 111.

4. Kelsey, *Psychology*, 146.

5. S. Augustini, *Retractationum* I.13.7, in *Patrologiae Latinae* 32 (1877), cols. 604–5, in Kelsey, *Psychology*, 146.

Chapter 14: Healing Gets Lost in Chaos: The Barbarian at the Gate

1. William A. Herr, *This Our Church* (Chicago: Thomas More Press, 1986), 46.

2. Ibid., 124–25.

3. Ibid.

Chapter 15: Healing Prayer Is Elevated Out of Reach

1. Technically termed *ex opere operato*.

2. Anne L. Barstow, *Married Priests and the Reforming Papacy: The Eleventh-Century Debates* (New York: Edwin Mellen Press, 1982), 35.

3. William A. Clebsch and Charles R. Jaekle, *Pastoral Care in Historical Perspective* (New York: Harper Torchbook, 1967), 156 (no. 25), 158 (no. 46) and 159 (no. 57), 160 (no. 67).

4. Frank C. Darling, *Christian Healing in the Middle Ages and Beyond* (Boulder, Colo.: Vista Publications, 1990), 138.

5. Bruno S. James, "Saint Bernard of Clairvaux: an Essay in Biography" in Darling, *Christian Healing*, 139–40.

Chapter 16: The Royal Touch

1. Marc Bloch, *The Royal Touch* (New York: Dorset Press, 1989).

2. Ibid., 47.

3. Ibid., 56.

4. Ibid., 65.

5. Ibid., 204.

6. Ibid., 212.

7. Ibid., 180.

8. Ibid., 170.

9. Ibid., 219–20. In 1702 Queen Anne came to power and held healing services with a simplified rite. But then the practice again died when she died (1714). King George I, brought over to assume the kingship from Hanover, Germany, never again attempted to resume royal healing services.

10. Ibid., 188.

Chapter 17: The Protestant Reformation and the Further Decline of Healing

1. Calvin, *Institutes*, b. 4, ch. 19, sect. 18.

2. Ibid., sects. 19 and 21.

3. William DeArteaga, *Quenching the Spirit: Discover the REAL Spirit Behind the Charismatic Controversy* (Lake Mary, Fla.: Creation House, 1992), 85. I would recommend reading this book for its extensive sections on the influences leading to the decline of the healing ministry.

Chapter 18: The Enlightenment and Dispensationalism: The Final Blows

1. Barclay, *The Gospel of Matthew*. v.

2. Ibid., 35.

3. There are notable exceptions, such as Jim Wallis, the evangelical founder of *Sojourners* magazine and the Sojourners community in Washington, D. C., who emphasizes evangelical teaching together with a peace and justice ministry. Wallis has written several influential books, such as *The Call to Conversion: Recovering the Gospel for These Times* (San Francisco: Harper & Row, 1981); and *Faith Works: Lessons from the Life of an Activist Preacher* (New York: Random House, 2000).

4. *The Harper Collins Encyclopedia of Catholicism* (New York: HarperCollins Publishers, 1995), 201.

5. Rudolf Bultmann, "A Reply to the Thesis of J. Schniewind," in *Kerygma and Myth: A Theological Debate*, ed. Hans Werner Bartsch, trans. R. H. Fuller (London: SPCK, 1957).

Chapter 19: Expectant Faith Remains in the People

1. Bert Ghezzi, *Mystics and Miracles* (Chicago: Loyola Press, 2002), 155–60.

2. It is interesting to note that the same dream is told about St. Francis of Assisi holding up the Basilica!

3. Ghezzi, *Mystics and Miracles*, 91.

4. Ibid., 93.

5. Francis MacNutt, *Healing*, Silver Anniversary ed. (1974; reprint, Notre Dame, Ind.: Ave Maria Press, 1999), 263.

6. Ghezzi, *Mystics and Miracles*, 117–23.

7. Ibid., 31–38.

8. Ibid., 149–54.

9. Ibid., 5–10.

10. Ibid., 173.

11. Ibid., 140–41.

12. Ibid., 76.

13. A friary was a building where friars, such as Franciscans and Dominicans, lived—as distinct from a monastery where monks, such as Benedictines, dwelt. Monks lived in only one place and had a "vow of stability," while friars could move from place to place.

14. *Magnificat*, 18 March 2002, 256.

15. Evely, *The Gospels Without Myth*, 25.

16. Kathryn Kuhlmann in those days (along with Oral Roberts) was the best-known American in the healing ministry.

17. On this subject—on how the Pentecostal-charismatic renewal has exploded until the new centers of Christianity will be in Asia and Africa, rather than in Rome and Germany—I would recommend reading Philip Jenkins's *The Next Christendom*.

Chapter 20: Fires Start (and Are Put Out)

1. You can read the life of Blumhardt in Friederich Zuendel's *The Awakening: One Man's Battle with Darkness* (Farmington, Pa.: Plough Publishing House, 2000). The facts in this chapter are taken from this book.

2. Ibid., 103.

3. Ibid., 107.

4. Ibid., 102–3.

5. For this aspect of Jonathan Edwards's life, refer to DeArteaga, *Quenching the Spirit*, 32–44.

6. Ibid., 45–55.

7. Ibid., 114–17.

8. "Then let the doctor take over—the Lord created him too—do not let him leave you, for you need him. There are times when good health depends on doctors" (Ecclesiasticus 38:12–13, NJB). Otherwise known as the Book of Sirach, this book is in the Apocrypha.

9. DeArteaga, *Quenching the Spirit*, 120–23.

10. Ibid., 117–20.

11. Ibid., 120.

12. Ibid., 123–26.

13. Ibid., 125–42.

14. Ibid., 130.

15. Ibid., 134–39.

16. Morton T. Kelsey, *Healing and Christianity* (New York: Harper & Row, 1973), 224. Fortunately, this is changing. *A Time to Heal* (London: Church House Publishing, 2000), a report for the Anglican Communion, is dedicated to the recovery of the healing ministry among Anglicans and is sponsored by the English House of Bishops.

17. William DeArteaga believes that this blockage comes from the spirit of the Pharisees, which afflicts the Church in every age (compare *Quenching the Spirit*).

18. John W. Gardner, *Self-Renewal: The Individual and the Innovative Society* (New York: W. W. Norton, 1981).

19. Ibid., 73.

20. The report on this international gathering is contained in *Prayer for Healing*, published by ICCRS, Palazzo della Cancelleria, 00120 Vatican City, Europe, 2003.

21. Teresa Malcolm, "Family Assists Others in Memory of Eric," *National Catholic Reporter*, 4 June 2004, 10.

Chapter 21: Pentecost Returns: The Twentieth Century

1. Mark Galli, "Revival at Cane Ridge," *Christian History* 14, no. 45: 11.

2. Ibid., 14.

3. Ibid.

4. Jenkins, *The Next Christendom*, 10.

5. A question remains, of course, about how deeply Christian the United States is. And yet visitors from the United Kingdom and the Continent have often remarked to me how amazed they are at how different the religious climate is in the United States, compared to the post-Christian apathy of Europe.

6. Timothy K. Beougher, "Did You Know," *Christian History* 14, no. 45: 3.

7. Ibid., 3.

8. Vinson Synan, *The Century of the Holy Spirit: 100 Years of Pentecostal and Charismatic Renewal* (Nashville: Thomas Nelson, 2001), 1.

9. It is also significant that in the Roman Catholic tradition, these outbreaks of spiritual experience and healing happen to insignificant people (according to the world's values) in out of the way places. In Lourdes, France, Mary, the Mother of God, is said to have appeared to a poor, uneducated girl, Bernadette of Soubiroux, in 1858. Lourdes is a small town in the Pyrenees. Since then countless streams of pilgrims have come to be healed in the spring that appeared at the site.

10. There are many accounts of the Azusa Street Revival. One, succinct and well-written, is Harvey Cox's "The Fire Falls in Los Angeles" in *Fire from Heaven*, 45–65.

11. Ibid., 59.

12. Ibid., 61.

13. Ibid., 105.

14. Ibid., 138.

Chapter 22: Charismatic Renewal and the Third Wave

1. Dennis J. Bennett, *Nine O'Clock in the Morning* (Gainesville, Fla.: Bridge-Logos, 1970).

2. I prayed for the release of the Holy Spirit in my own life in August of that same year.

3. John Wimber and Kevin Springer, *Power Healing* (San Francisco: HarperCollins, 1987).

4. An excellent extended account of this worldwide movement is Dr. Vinson Synan's *The Century of the Holy Spirit*.

5. If you are interested in this crucial subject, you might read my book *Homosexuality: Can it be Healed?* Available from Christian Healing Ministries, P.O. Box 9520, Jacksonville, FL 32208.

6. See my book *Deliverance from Evil Spirits*.

7. David Barrett, "The Worldwide Holy Spirit Renewal," in Synan, *The Century of the Holy Spirit*, 381–85.

8. Ibid., 383.

Chapter 23: The New Face of Christianity

1. Jenkins, *The Next Christendom*, 94–95.

2. Ibid., 64.

3. Ibid., 69.

4. Ibid., 74.

5. Ibid., 12.

6. Ibid., 3.

7. Ibid., 8.

8. Ibid., 125.

9. Ibid., 65.

10. Ibid., 49.

11. Ibid., 59–60.

Chapter 24: Will We Remain on the Sidelines?

1. There are now many excellent books written on healing and some also on deliverance. The ministry we founded, Christian Healing Ministries, has a website (www.christian healingmin.org) and a small mail-order bookstore to help you out if need be.

BIBLIOGRAPHY

Amorth, Gabriele. *An Exorcist Tells His Story*. San Francisco: Ignatius Press, 1999.

Barclay, William. *The Gospel of Matthew*. Vol. 2. Rev. ed. Philadelphia: Westminster Press, 1975.

Barstow, Anne L. *Married Priests and the Reforming Papacy: The Eleventh-Century Debates*. New York: Edwin Mellen Press, 1982.

Bartsch, Hans Werner, ed. *Kerygma and Myth: A Theological Debate*. Translated by R. H. Fuller. London: SPCK, 1957.

Beougher, Timothy K. "Did You Know?" *Christian History* 14, no. 45: 3

Bloch, Marc. *The Royal Touch*. New York: Dorset Press, 1989.

Calvin. *Institutes*.

Clebsch, William A., and Charles R. Jaekle. *Pastoral Care in Historical Perspective*. New York: Harper Torchbook, 1967.

Cox, Harvey. *Fire from Heaven: The Rise of Pentecostal Spirituality and the Reshaping of Religion in the Twenty-First Century*. Reading, Mass.: Addison-Wesley, 1995.

Darling, Frank C. *Biblical Healing: Hebrew and Christian Roots*. Boulder, Colo.: Vista Publications,1989.

_____. *Christian Healing in the Middle Ages and Beyond*. Boulder, Colo.: Vista Publications, 1990.

DeArteaga, William. *Quenching the Spirit: Discover the REAL Spirit Behind the Charismatic Controversy*. Lake Mary, Fla.: Creation House, 1992.

Dossey, Larry, M.D. *Prayer Is Good Medicine*. San Francisco: Harper-Collins, 1996.

Evely, Louis. *The Gospels Without Myth*. New York: Doubleday, 1970.

Frost, Evelyn. *Christian Healing*. London: A. R. Mowbray, 1940.

Galli, Mark. "Revival at Cane Ridge." *Christian History* 14, no. 45: 11.

Gardner, John W. *Self-Renewal: The Individual and the Innovative Society*. New York: W. W. Norton, 1981.

Ghezzi, Bert. *Mystics and Miracles*. Chicago: Loyola Press, 2002.

Glasser, William, M.D. *Reality Therapy: A New Approach to Psychiatry*. New York: Harper & Row, 1965.

Hamman, André. *Baptism: Ancient Liturgies and Patristic Texts*. Staten Island, N.Y.: Alba House, 1967.

The HarperCollins Encyclopedia of Catholicism. New York: Harper-Collins, 1995.

Herr, William A. *This Our Church*. Chicago, Ill.: Thomas More Press, 1986.

Jenkins, Philip. *The Next Christendom: The Coming of Global Christianity*. New York: Oxford University Press, 2002.

Kelsey, Morton T. *Healing and Christianity*. New York: Harper & Row, 1973.

_____. *Psychology, Medicine and Christian Healing*. San Francisco: Harper & Row, 1988.

MacMullen, Ramsay. *Christianizing the Roman Empire: A.D. 100–400*. New Haven and London: Yale University Press, 1984.

MacNutt, Francis. *Deliverance from Evil Spirits: A Practical Manual*. Grand Rapids: Chosen Books, 1995.

_____. *Healing*. 1974. Reprint, Notre Dame, Ind.: Ave Maria Press, 1999.

_____. *The Power to Heal*. Notre Dame, Ind.: Ave Maria Press, 1977.

McDonnell, Kilian, and George T. Montague. *Christian Initiation and Baptism in the Holy Spirit: Evidence from the First Eight Centuries*. 2d ed. Collegeville, Minn.: Liturgical Press, 1994.

_____. *Fanning the Flame: What Does Baptism in the Holy Spirit Have to Do with Christian Initiation?* Collegeville, Minn.: Liturgical Press, 1991.

Magnificat, 18 March 2002.

Noonan, John T. Jr. *Contraception: A History of Its Treatment by the Catholic Theologians and Canonists*. New York: Mentor-Omega Books, 1965.

Story of a Soul: The Autobiography of St. Thérèse of Lisieux. 3rd ed. Translated by John Clarke, O.C.D. Washington, D.C.: ICS Publications, 1996.

Synan, Vinson. *The Century of the Holy Spirit: 100 Years of Pentecostal and Charismatic Renewal*. Nashville: Thomas Nelson, 2001.

Talbert, Charles H. *Reading Luke*. New York: Crossroad, 1992.

Wimber, John, and Kevin Springer. *Power Healing*. San Francisco: HarperCollins, 1987.

Wright, N. T. *The Challenge of Jesus*. Downers Grove, Ill.: InterVarsity Press, 1999.

Zuendel, Friedrich. *The Awakening: One Man's Battle with Darkness*. Farmington, Pa.: Plough Publishing House, 2000.

INDEX

241

Francis S. MacNutt was born in 1925. Ten days before entering medical school he was drafted into the Army and served as a surgical technician during World War II. After receiving a B.A. from Harvard and M.F.A. from Catholic University of America, he studied to be a Roman Catholic priest and was ordained in 1956. He received a Ph.D. in theology from the Aquinas Institute of Theology, where he was then appointed to teach homiletics.

Francis experienced the baptism of the Holy Spirit in 1967 and learned about praying for healing from the Reverend Tommy Tyson and Agnes Sanford. He was one of the first Roman Catholics to be involved in the charismatic renewal. Entering the full-time preaching ministry, he began traveling all over the world and writing books on the subject of healing. His book *Healing* (Ave Maria Press; reissued by Creation House) has sold more than a million copies in the United States alone. His five other books on healing include *Deliverance from Evil Spirits* (Chosen Books).

In 1975 Francis met Judith Sewell in Jerusalem, where she was a missionary. Five years later they married and settled in Clearwater, Florida. He and Judith co-authored *Praying for Your Unborn Child* (Doubleday). Together they founded Christian Healing Ministries and, taking their two children with them, traveled widely, speaking as a team. In 1987 they moved the ministry base to Jacksonville, Florida, invited there by the Episcopal Diocese of Florida. The teaching ministry is carried out through conferences, seminars, books, tapes, and speaking engagements by the MacNutts and staff members as well as invited speakers.

In addition to praying and teaching, CHM has established relationships with other Christian ministries and counselors around the world for networking and referral purposes.

For more information, contact:

Christian Healing Ministries, Inc.
P.O. Box 9520
Jacksonville, FL 32208
(904) 765–3332
www.christianhealingmin.org

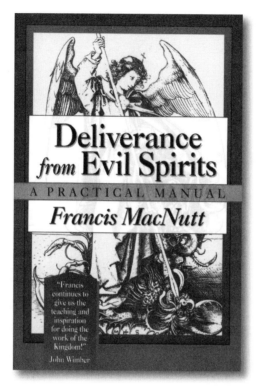